ALONE
but not lonely

Alone, But Not Lonely

Thoughts for the single, widowed,
or divorced woman

by Wayne J. Anderson, Ph.D.

Published by
Deseret Book Company
Salt Lake City, Utah
1973

ISBN Number 0-87747-496-6
Library of Congress Number 73-77832

Copyright 1973
by
Deseret Book Company

CONTENTS

PART FIVE: CHOOSING A MATE

PART SIX: GUIDELINES TO CONFIDENT LIVING

Foreword

This book was written as the result of classes and interviews with hundreds of single women who have repeatedly asked, "When are you going to put the things we have talked about into book form?"

The final motivation was provided by Wm. James Mortimer of Deseret Book Company, who encouraged its publication.

It must be understood that no book can be written about the single woman only. She is not an entity apart, and she can't be separated from society or the things that all people do, need, and think about. Like all of us, she interacts with the living world, influences others, and is in turn influenced by those around her.

Consequently, the concepts presented here are directed toward every single or married individual who is interested in considering the suggested guidelines for confident living.

It is addressed primarily to single, divorced, and widowed women because those I have counseled with have asked for it, and also because they wanted me to put some of their thinking into the book. Thus it is a joint effort, written by the author and the single women he has met with.

Finally, it should be made clear that this book is not intended to take the place of counseling. Rather, like other written materials, it is designed to stimulate thinking and suggest guidelines to the reader.

Acknowledgments

I owe a debt of gratitude to the many single women who have met with me in counseling sessions throughout the years. Their thoughts constitute a major part of this book.

I am also grateful to my wife, Elise, and our children, Annette, Cherie Wayne, Jim, Julie Gay, and Jill for their encouragement and support.

My special thanks go to Jill, who has gone the extra mile in helping me. She has patiently deciphered my handwriting and put it into neat typescript, and her suggestions for improving the manuscript have been invaluable.

—Wayne J. Anderson

PART ONE

Loneliness can
be overcome

1

Why Be Lonely?

Feeling lonely is a common human problem. It is the rare individual who has not had feelings of loneliness at least once in life. Moreover, such feelings strike people at all age levels and often without advance notice. Here are some typical comments of lonely people:

Terry, a college student, said, "Although I live in a dormitory with eight hundred other men, no one will talk to me because I have a known prison record. I might as well be alone on a deserted island."

Becky, a high school senior, remarked bitterly, "I just can't talk to Mom and Dad, and the kids at school are always putting me down. I'm so lonely I could die."

Sandra, a widow, sighed as she declared, "I've found myself becoming physically affectionate with a man I don't really like, just to avoid my heavy feelings of loneliness."

Steve, a bachelor, complained, "After work I'm so lonely I just don't know what to do with myself. I can't seem to make any friends with whom I can relax and talk."

Over half of the people interviewed in preparing material for this book considered loneliness as an obstacle to well being; the things that they most frequently gave as causes of loneliness were:
· The lack of a closely knit family group
· Having no friends who really care
· Having no satisfying social activities
· The feeling that life has passed them by
· Retreating into self-pity
· Not feeling needed
· Having no sense of involvement with others
· Having no special goals in life
A careful look at these reasons reveals that the mere presence of people will not banish loneliness from our lives. Some people who are alone are not lonely, and others who are not alone are lonely. In other words, it's possible to feel lonely in a busy supermarket or a jammed football stadium. This is so because the feeling of loneliness comes from within and is related to our individual state of mind; thus, we are the only ones who can eventually dispel our loneliness. Others may help and provide us with things, and others may shape circumstances to help us combat loneliness, but unless we develop a positive state of mind, such efforts will be of small significance.

Overcoming Loneliness

Are there specific things we can do to rid ourselves of a feeling of loneliness? Individuals who have succeeded say there are. The following are some of their suggestions.

Each of us is part of the living world, so we must play the game of life. Standing on the sidelines and complaining helps no one.

We should try to entertain interesting thoughts and do interesting things, if we desire to be interesting to others.

Other people will not be interested in us unless we show interest in them.

We can enjoy being alone by developing such hobbies as collecting things—from stamps to seashells; playing or listening to music; creating things by painting, sculpting, or writing; or making things, such as clothes, beads, or decorations.

We can enjoy being with others by being good listeners, by getting out of our shell and speaking cheerfully to people; by joining classes or groups that do things; and by being interested in others.

Reading about and observing others who seem to have conquered feelings of loneliness can also be helpful.

Recently a woman who evidently lived alone and enjoyed life sent a small note to the editor of our local newspaper that subsequently caused much favorable comment throughout the town. She wrote:

My morning tasks were finished, and my wee house was in order, so I sat down and played the piano a bit. The door was open, letting in the bright sunshine and fragrant air. As I played I could see the branches of the trees sway in harmonious rhythm. I played a favorite piece and my canary caroled a shrill obbligato. I played on until the tinkle of the tiny bell over my mail chute told me the postman had come.

As I read my mail, my canary stopped warbling, and a feeling of great peace came over me. Walking to my front door, I looked up at the blue sky and gave thanks to my Creator for the privilege of living in such a wonderful world.

—Pat R.

It would be much easier for all of us to overcome feelings of loneliness if we could feel like Pat, if we could enjoy the beauty of the world, be thankful for the gift of life, and share our happy thoughts with others.

Other suggestions for overcoming loneliness that might be more closely related to your specific situation are given in subsequent chapters.

Summary

Being alone and loneliness are not the same.
The mere presence of people will not dispel
    loneliness.
Joy comes from within.
We must play the game of life. Standing on the
    sidelines won't help.
If we like people, people will like us.
We should remember, as Robert Browning said,
    "God's in his heaven, and all's right with
    the world."

PART TWO

When one's mate passes
to the other side

2

Left All Alone?

A woman who had recently lost her mate said, "During the memorial services when your departed husband is eulogized by the speakers, and the beautiful music comforts your grieving heart, you feel a glow of satisfaction over having been the faithful wife of such a good man. Your serenity continues when multitudes of your friends and relatives accompany you to the cemetery and a beautiful dedicatory prayer is spoken over the final resting place of your mate's earthly body. This state of euphoria continues as relatives and friends gather at your home, bringing with them delicious foods and sharing thoughts about your future.

"But when the last guest has said good-bye and you are sitting quietly in your memory-filled home, you suddenly feel all alone and a thought intrudes and upsets your calm self-assurance: 'How can I manage to continue living and meet the constant challenges of life without my husband?' You think further, 'My marriage was a twenty-four-hour-a-day job that involved my heart and my mind and embraced my work, my social life, my private life, and my church activity. How can I possibly reorganize my day-to-day living and keep on doing the things I know I should?' Finding how doesn't usually come from the sympathy of well-meaning friends. But sometimes the answer does come when you talk to wives who have undergone the same experience."

To help you find the answer to the question of how, this discussion will describe how others have met the same challenges you now face.

In discussing this question with many other wives who have lost their husbands, the writer has heard three fundamental approaches mentioned over and over again.

1. *Those wives who have learned how to adjust do not consider their husband dead, nor are they concerned about his welfare.* This enables them to meet the first part of their challenge and to close their minds to worries about him.

"My husband has just been transferred to a place where his Heavenly Father has greater need for him," said one sweet sister.

"I am grateful that my Harry was allowed to leave his ailing body and go where his spirit could serve without being burdened by the ills of the flesh," commented another.

"Don't feel sorry for me or my Oliver," smiled a tiny housewife. "He was too good for this world, so he got promoted."

"I'm sure everyone on the other side has been made happier by my Jack's sunny disposition," said another. "It will be fun when I can join him."

Such expressions surely make "the other side" seem a happy place, don't they? Such a belief should also give the individual a feeling of peace about her husband.

"I agree," you say. "Sure, my husband's all right, but what about me? What can I do on *this* side? It's still difficult to be left alone."

This brings us to the second approach to the challenge.

2. *Those wives who have learned how to adjust are aware*

*that now is the time to redefine their relationships with their
Father in heaven and with his Son, Jesus Christ.* They realize
that each woman, be she single, married, divorced, or
widowed, is a daughter of God and has her own special
role to play in this life. They know also that going through
God's earthly school and learning how to return to him
must be done on an individual basis whether the woman
is with or without a husband.

Church members who understand clearly this part of
God's plan have said:

"My first great blessing was being born, so I could go
through God's earthly school."

"My present job is to love God and serve his children
in this world."

"I know God hasn't forgotten me because he also
takes care of the fowls of the air and the lilies of the field."

"God is my Father, and I can talk to him without
worrying that he will criticize me or gossip about my
problems."

These daughters of God feel that he loves them and
sent his Son to teach them how to find eternal life.

How do you feel? Do you know he loves you as an
individual and is always mindful of you?

If you do, then it's time to consider the third approach.

3. *Those wives who have learned how to adjust know how
to find their way to eternal life with God, their Father, and
his Son, Jesus Christ.*

"I feel I am traveling closer to God when I try to serve
his children," said a Woman of the Year.

"Drawing close to God in prayer has helped me to
understand that I can be reunited with my husband and
with God, my Father, in the future life," observed another.

"How can I find my way back to God's dwelling
place?" asked a stately woman. "By loving him and trying
to be like him and radiating that same love to the world."

These women have caught the spirit that will guide
them on the road back to God. Each of us can do the same

thing. But we will need to use faith plus works. Use of either one without the other will cause us to lose our direction and wind up in confusion. On the other hand, combining faith with works will enable us to meet each new day with a positive attitude.

Avoiding Loneliness

The best way to build a new life is to start immediately. Sitting around feeling sorry for one's self will make things worse.

One woman suggested that you can start with a positive act at the funeral home. She said, "When your friends come to console you and sign their names in your guest book, do something to shape your future positively by having them sign a calendar appointment book instead, and designate a future date when they will remember you with a card, a phone call, or a visit. If you do this, even before you return home, you will have future social contacts to look forward to."

Your first few days at home may go by without extreme difficulty because of numbness from shock or the inevitable number of things that must be done as a result of your husband's passing. However, when you get back to the routine things of life, such as sleeping, eating, and just keeping busy, you may have trouble.

Take, for example, getting sufficient sleep. If drinking warm milk and counting sheep doesn't help (experts say it doesn't), try some of the following things used by others to induce relaxation and sleep.

Arlene Dahl, widely known for her beauty, uses "a tepid bath filled with fragrant bubbles," or lies on a slant board, "which places your legs higher than your head."

Actresses Jennifer Jones and Gloria Swanson practice yoga. Bob Hope follows a nutritious diet and has a rubdown at bedtime.

Norman Vincent Peale empties his mind of all of the irritations of the day into an imaginary wastebasket, which helps him to relax and enjoy rest.

You will probably develop your own method of getting to sleep, but above all, don't fret if you find yourself shifting positions and awakening frequently. Studies show that it is not normal to "sleep like a log," and furthermore, many people catch little periods of snoozes interrupted by body movements until they drift into a deeper state of lethargy. Don't worry if you lie awake during certain periods of the night. Your body is still resting. Just assume that you will soon fall asleep again and chances are that you will.

Here's a suggested daily schedule to follow, which is printed here with the permission of a female colleague who combined the best ideas found in women's magazines during the last twenty years as the topic for her thesis to acquire a master's degree.

Daily Schedule

1. *Enjoy your breakfast.*

Now you are alone, you no longer need to engage in Spartan-like behavior and rise early and fix up to eat your morning meal. Unless you have a job, you can enjoy a leisurely breakfast in bed. (Even if you do work outside your home, getting up early enough to enjoy breakfast helps start the day right.)

Place your television set nearby and listen to the morning news. Scan the newspaper. Keep in touch and be a part of today's world.

Thank God that you have the privilege of enjoying another new day. And realize that you have an important role to play in building his kingdom.

2. *Practice the two double EE's necessary to efficient body functioning: enlightened eating and enlightened exercise.*

Observe the Word of Wisdom, shun liquor and tobacco, and use moderation in your eating habits. Control the eating of starchy foods and develop a nutritious, well-

balanced diet that you enjoy. If you feel the need to reduce, studies indicate that it is wise to eat small, frequent
meals and to avoid gnawing hunger by munching on car-
rots or celery strips.

Engage in body stimulating exercises you enjoy. Exercise should make you stretch your muscles and breathe
deeply. Find a daily exercise routine you enjoy. It need
not take the form of calisthenics. You might have fun and
benefit physically by walking, jogging, swimming, playing
games, such as tennis, golf, and bowling, or dancing.

3. *Package yourself attractively.*

You can look frumpish or fashionable, dowdy or
dashing; it all depends on you. It doesn't cost a fortune to
be well-dressed. Make a game of it and depend more on
ingenuity than money.

Learn to shop for bargains.

Find fun in coordinating clothes.

Throw away that old dress you dislike!

Wear colors that lift your spirits.

Put yourself on a solid foundation by wearing comfortable and attractive shoes. (Buy two pairs at a time and
alternate wearing them during the day.)

4. *Begin each day feeling you have important things to do.*

Realize that your life is affecting others, so exercise
true womanhood by giving your gifts of love, compassion,
and spirituality to those around you.

5. *Fit brief rest periods into your daily schedule.*

Avoid the frayed nerves and emotional instability
that accompany fatigue.

6. *Set up a daily goal.*

This might vary from filling so many pages in a
scrapbook to visiting a sick friend. If you enroll in a crafts

class, take music lessons, join a health club, or whatever, other people will help you meet these daily goals.

7. *Try to observe something amusing or pleasant each day.*

Put it in your diary or tell your friends about it.

8. *If you have a tendency to worry, set aside 15 minutes each day for this purpose.*

For example, worry from 9:00 until 9:15 A.M. This way you will control it. If you find yourself becoming depressed, *do something.*
· Read a book
· Turn to Psalm 66
· Write a friend
· Bake some cookies
· Make a dress
· Plant some flowers
· Rearrange furniture
· Redecorate a room
· Invite a friend over
If all these things fail to help, do as the old popular song advised:
"Put on your hat; lock up your flat.
Get out and get under the (moon) sun."
Or go shopping, take a trip, or move to a new location.

9. *Constantly remind yourself how wonderful it is to be a daughter of God and thank him each day for the continued opportunity to learn more in the school of life.*

Your Social Life

Some people say their social life makes them feel imprisoned. Others in similar circumstances are joyful. This is true; your social life can make you feel like you are in prison or paradise: it depends upon your attitude.

It goes without saying, that taking a church job and being active in related activities will provide some respite from loneliness. But what can one do between church meetings?

How about entertaining at home? Getting ready for a party can keep you busy doing pleasant things, such as fixing up the living room, baking cookies, and planning interesting activities for your guests to enjoy.

To top it off, it might help to make or buy yourself a colorful hostess gown, put it on, and greet your guests with a smile.

Whom can you invite? Anyone—young students, couples, unattached men, people who are fun to be with. If you plan things right, you will become known as the "hostess with the mostes'," and people will jump at any invitation to your home.

Your social activities outside your home can be many and varied. The important thing is to do what you enjoy, not what you think you should enjoy. These things may take the form of attending concerts, movies, sports activities, or lectures, or participating in bowling, golf, tennis, swimming, horseback riding or what have you.

Summary

Other women who have gone through the experience say that adjusting to the loss of your husband is easier if you—
— realize he has been called to another sphere of activity,
— remember that you have an individual relationship with God,
— follow the path of service that leads to eternal life with God.
The best way to cope with daily living is to have a positive attitude and keep busy.
God loves you and wants you to be happy!

3

Challenges Confronting
the One-Parent Family

Women who have been left with children say that if your husband passes away and leaves you alone with young children, you have the same challenges to meet as mentioned in the previous chapter, plus a few more.

Let's assume, as suggested, that you have found your own inner peace. Have your children found theirs? Perhaps. Children have great faith and usually recover quickly from emotional hurts. But not having lived very many years in this world, they often need explanations of new experiences they can't comprehend.

It may be that your youngsters initially showed great understanding at the services for their father and even told their friends, "Our dad's gone to Heavenly Father and we'll see him again someday."

But in the days to come when the harsh reality of living without their dad hits them, they may become depressed and begin to complain.

So, what do you do or say if your five-year-old Billy suddenly sobs, "Why did Heavenly Father take Dad

19

away? I want my dad. Golly, Mom, I don't think God is very nice. I hate him."

What do you do? Lash back angrily with, "Billy! Don't you dare talk about God that way! You should be ashamed of yourself!"

Not if you can avoid it. Such a sharp rebuke would not drive Billy's anger away. In fact, it might reinforce it.

Better to take your son in your arms, comfort him, and reply, "Billy, I miss Dad too, and I don't know just why God took him away at this time, but I do know something."

"What's that?" asks Billy.

"That God loves us, and as our Father in heaven, he will be with us and help us. Let me ask you a question. Do you believe I love you?"

"Of course!"

"Do you remember the day when I took a shiny knife away from you? Do you think it was because I didn't love you?"

"Well, I suppose it was because you didn't want me to cut myself."

"Right! Can you see then that when God took Daddy away, it didn't mean that he had stopped loving us?"

"Well, maybe."

"He probably had a reason for taking your father now, a reason that we can't understand. But I'm sure we will someday."

Such a conversation might calm Billy down and help him to understand God's plan, and again it might not. However, it will give him something to think about and will help bring him to greater understanding.

In the days, months, and years to come, you will probably need to be a source of faith to all of your children, so do your best to treat their doubts with patience and understanding.

For example, your younger daughter may feel insecure because she cannot comprehend the meaning of death; she may shriek in terror every time you leave the house, thinking that you might never come back. A little thing like pointing to the clock and saying, "Lucy, I am going to the corner store for some groceries and I'll be back when the big hand is on twelve and the little one is on three," might ease the situation.

Another precaution to prevent childhood anxiety, if it is necessary to have a baby-sitter, is to use the services of a girl whom your children already know and feel comfortable with.

If you have teenagers in the family, try to encourage them to discuss their feelings about their father with you. And if his loss has made you feel depressed, let them know that your emotional state at the time has not lessened your love for them. Some wives say they cannot bear the emotional strain that comes from talking about their late husband. But they have also noticed that avoiding such discussion puts a strain on everyone. It is better to try to recall and relive happy experiences when he was alive. If your children join naturally in such discussions, they will remember the happiness their father gave them, and the reality that he is still living somewhere else will be easier for them to accept.

These conversations can draw the family closer together and help develop in its members the desire to live as happily as possible until a reunion with their father takes place.

Performing Family Chores

Many widows report that they soon realize that their husband peformed many little tasks that were taken for granted, and with his passing these tasks have fallen on their shoulders. Try to avoid letting this happen to you, when you have children. It will do you, them, and the entire family good if they all share in the performance of necessary tasks. The trick is knowing how to get your children to perform them willingly and happily.

Using direct confrontation seldom works. Avoid say-

ing such things as, "Joe, you're big enough to do some of
the things your father used to do. Now, get busy, can't you
see I've got my hands full?" This would probably bring
about stubborn resistance or unwilling compliance.

More cheerful cooperation will occur if you can build
the feeling in Joe's and the other children's minds that the
home you live in belongs to all of them, and that chores
are a group responsibility. Nevertheless, it must be em-
phasized that just telling your sons and daughters this fact
has little meaning. You must demonstrate it in action.
How? Here are some suggestions you might consider.

Children should be allowed a voice in how the home
is decorated. Let them choose the colors and furniture for
their own rooms, and respect their opinions regarding
arrangements in family centers, such as the living room.

Afford them the freedom to put up posters, proverbs,
or whatever they desire on their walls. It is much better
ror your daughter to have the satisfaction of seeing a religious sampler that she embroidered in Primary hanging
on the wall than to buy an expensive, framed wall hanging.

It is also important that each family member has
sufficient living space. If possible, every child should have
a room, a space, a corner, or, if nothing else, a chest of
drawers with which he may do as he pleases—namely,
engage in self-expression.

Building Family Unity

Building a united family presents a constant challenge. Some of the following activities might help.

Develop family rituals. These are part of the cement
that unites a family. Family prayers and blessing meals
with each member taking a turn as voice may help build
a oneness of feeling. Birthday cakes with candles to blow
out and wishes to be made can also help. Making the
Sabbath day special and attending church together develops unity of purpose.

Weekly family home evenings offer many opportunities for family members to understand and appreciate one another. Many parents feel that the home evening presents an excellent opportunity to recognize children's achievements and discuss family problems and projects.

Have you thought about developing a family organization? One mother even went so far as to organize her group as the Jones Family, Incorporated, and gave each member a title and voting shares of stock in the corporation. Their corporate structure took this form:

The Jones Family, Incorporated

	Voting Shares of Stock
Chairman of the Board: Mother	25
Executive Vice-President: Ned (14)	25
Secretary-Treasurer: Mary (12)	15
Superintendent of Buildings and Grounds: Tim (10)	15
Chief Messenger: Bob (7)	15
Official Sunshine Dispenser and Tidy-upper: Becky (5)	15

The mother who reported this family's experience said giving each member a title, rotating jobs, and voting on family problems and projects got the family work done more happily and effectively.

Although you may be busy, try to schedule your time so you can play games and have fun with your children. Ping-Pong in the basement and volleyball, badminton, and basketball in the backyard are more fun if mother takes part. On wintry evenings, engaging in word games and getting around the piano to sing will liven up the entire family.

It seems unnecessary to suggest that you lead out in encouraging your children to participate in church social activities, as most mothers do this.

Paid entertainment can be rejuvenating too, if selected with care. Attending a concert or a sports event as a family group may motivate your children to achieve new goals.

An important part of family fun is to cultivate a sense of humor. We should all try to laugh at our own mistakes and let our children know we are human. You will probably also make them aware that you occasionally need a night out with another adult or adults and that this in no way diminishes your love for them.

Managing Family Finances

Money! Money! There's never enough!

So say many mothers who have been left to manage without their husbands. Managing your family dollars can indeed become a headache if you have no planned guidelines. On the other hand, sound money management can pay handsome dividends in individual and collective growth of family members.

Here are management suggestions that should produce dividends rather than headaches.

1. *Determine your gross income (the money you receive from all sources) and decide if it will cover your family's needs and plans.*

Your possible sources of income might include a pension, Social Security checks, life insurance, interest on stocks and bonds, or savings. Will the total sum maintain the style of life you and your children want? If so, decide as a family group how you will allocate it. If not, go to step two.

2. *Explore ways to augment your income.*

The supposedly easy way out would be to ask for handouts from the Church welfare plan or your county welfare department. But handouts often weaken self-pride, self-respect, and independence. Nevertheless, these organizations have been set up to aid you if you have need, so approach them on a businesslike basis, with your head held high.

First, let's take your approach to the Church for participation in the welfare plan. Consult with your bishop and ask him what services you and your children can render in exchange for food, clothing, or cash. Unless your health or other problems make your rendering service impossible, he will work out something for you to do. Otherwise, he will consider helping you anyway.

Similarly, your county welfare department stands ready to help with something besides handouts. Take advantage of their family guidance and counseling clinic. They can give you information about various forms of federal aid for the single parent. Such services include educational grants, assistance in buying a home, and, in some instances, free child care while you finish your education. If you qualify, they will also arrange a monthly income for you under the Aid for Families with Dependent Children program. The welfare department will also be happy to refer you to psychological and medical agencies that can provide assistance.

Of course the Church is also equipped to provide these services through its Health Services and Social Services.

If you are an active Church member, you will undoubtedly want to work through your bishop to meet your needs. However, there is no harm in learning of the services that your government will provide you. And you may move closer to your goals if you can receive a combination of help from both the church and the government.

Other ways you might consider to augment your income would include taking a full- or part-time job, encouraging the older children to work part-time, or working as a family group to earn additional income. If you live on a farm, many possibilities will present themselves. If you are city dwellers, you may find companies that would be glad to have your family do piecework for them at home.

3. *Make your financial watchword, "All for One and One for All."*

True, this statement is a tired cliché. But pulling together this way, if the proper spirit is present, develops a loyalty and cohesiveness in family units that is glorious to behold. Many families have reported that their happiest times occurred when they were struggling together to meet their economic needs.

4. *Always consult an attorney before undertaking any major financial projects.*

Most cities have a Legal Aid Society, which provides counsel free or for a nominal fee. If such is not available, ask around until you find an understanding attorney who has your interests at heart.

5. *Develop sound buying habits.*

Family members should shop around and compare prices, read labels, and learn to evaluate clothing materials and foods. If credit is used, it should be used wisely and never for impulsive buying. Money should be used for individual members' needs in such a way that a balance is achieved in maintaining individual identity and a group cooperative spirit.

6. *Have a financial plan or budget so you will know how your money is spent.*

Don't make this so tight that you have to account for every dime spent. If possible, arrange an allowance for each member that can be spent for needs and desires without making an accounting to the group.

7. *Remember: money itself is nothing. It is how it is spent that counts.*

Things of the Spirit

All parents who are active church workers try to keep constantly before their children the knowledge that each one of them is a child of God, and that their long-range common goal is to be united as a family in the celestial kingdom. Here are some of the things you might want to do to help you achieve this goal.

Have a family code of behavior. Impress upon your children that family members who are active in the

Church have no doubts as to what is right and wrong, and that their religious beliefs let them know that there are no "gray" shadings that color their moral codes—no opportunities for rationalization. Right and wrong are as clearly differentiated for them as night and day. Consequently, they should spend their energies striving to live right and not quibble about what is good or bad.

Help your children learn to give priority to the things of greatest value in life and to realize that feelings of personal worth and self-respect come from living lives of service and integrity rather than from the acquisition of material possessions.

Encourage all family members to keep actively engaged in church work. This will keep their testimonies strong and provide them with built-in spiritual stabilizers that will help them through trying times.

And keep before your children's minds and plant within their hearts that—

—they were sent here by God,

—they are going through his earthly school, and

—they will return to live with him if they exercise faith and works.

Summary

Explaining to our children the plan of life if their father or mother is called home will help them to feel more secure.

Trying to be calm and understanding and guiding them through emotional upsets will help our inner peace.

Teaching them to share family chores will lighten our load.

Holding family home evenings and observing interesting family rituals will build unity.

Using wisdom in managing the family's money will help us to avoid many tensions.

Keeping before children that our common goal is to be united as a family in God's kingdom now and forever will help promote spirituality.

PART 3

Divorce—
before and after

4

Information About
Divorce Procedures

"It cost me forty dollars to consult an attorney. And I was so mixed up I didn't know what was going on. When my friends found out, they made things worse by constantly phoning to see how 'poor Bonnie' (I) was doing."

Getting a divorce can be a traumatic experience at best, and when little is understood about divorce procedures, the resulting involvements can become emotionally shattering.

In order to help you avoid these additional tensions if you have decided on divorce, the necessary legal steps are outlined below. A clear understanding of what lies ahead should help allay the anxiety that comes from facing the unknown and also make it easier to bear the emotional pressures that will follow.

Even though you have made up your mind to seek divorce, you should avoid taking any steps in that direction until you have consulted an attorney. Why is this so important? Basically because you must acquaint yourself with your legal rights concerning the following questions:

Have I resided in the state long enough to be eligible to file for a divorce?

Do I have legal grounds for divorce? (These vary from state to state.)

Can I qualify to receive alimony?

What is the law regarding child support?

How is custody of the children determined?

How are visitation rights to the children arranged?

If you have had no previous contact with lawyers, you may need help in choosing one. If The Church of Jesus Christ of Latter-day Saints has a referral service in your area, go there first. If none is available, contact the Legal Aid Society, which has offices in most big cities. Their staff will direct you to a lawyer or advise you on legal procedures if you cannot afford to hire a lawyer. The Lawyer Referral Service, which the American Bar Association sponsors in nearly two hundred cities, is also a source of help. They will charge you about five dollars to determine if you have a case.

If you go to a private lawyer, he will proceed as follows: listen to your complaint, determine if you have grounds for divorce, and charge you somewhere between twenty-five and forty dollars for his advice.

If he decides you have legal grounds for divorce and you engage him to represent you, he will ask you to deposit a retainer (pay a sum of money in advance) to reimburse him for drawing up the necessary papers. Be sure to ask him how much his retainer is, as attorney fees vary from a low of one hundred dollars to a high of several hundred. The lawyer collects this money in advance because divorce clients often change their minds in midstream, drop the case, and assume they owe nothing because no legal steps were taken. Consequently, your lawyer wants assurance that he will be paid for work he has done, no matter what happens.

It must be mentioned that you and your husband are usually not allowed to share the same lawyer. Things seem to work out more satisfactorily when each partner is represented by his own attorney. This is true even though your husband in most cases pays the lawyers' and court costs.

If you engage a lawyer and are dissatisfied with his work, you may change to someone else. However, you will be obligated to pay your first lawyer for the time he has spent on the case.

Grounds for Divorce

One thing important to know about divorce law is that you and your husband cannot divorce without a lawsuit and sufficient legal grounds. In other words, it is not possible to shake hands and call your marriage off. Instead, one of you generally must be found guilty of a marital offense. This is usually necessary in divorce law even if you have no conflicts and agree privately that you no longer want to be married.

Before grounds for divorce are discussed, it should be stated that this court procedure of requiring a wrongdoer and an innocent party in each suit has been under fire for a long time. And to remedy this, California has pioneered with a new state divorce law enacted in 1969, which changed that state's procedure to a no-fault divorce system—irreconcilable differences, or the fact that the marriage is not working, now being the only grounds for divorce. The divorce courts have been renamed the family law department, and the term *divorce* has been replaced by the word *dissolution*. The word *plaintiff* has been changed to the *petitioner*, and the *defendant* is now known as the *respondent*. Alimony is called *spousal support*.

These changes in California have done away with the old divorce-court rancor; and if name-calling begins when child custody is considered, the law states that such evidence about misconduct must be limited, it may be heard in private, and the best interests of the child rather than the alleged unfitness of a parent should determine which partner will receive custody.

Some other states have been moving in this same direction with their divorce courts, so when you consult your lawyer, you should ask him if your area has a family court or some other modified system of procedure. If such divorce systems are not available, you will be faced with selecting grounds for divorce, which you may use if you have been a resident of the state for a specified length of time.

The most common (there are exceptions in a few states) grounds for divorce are:

1. *Adultery.* Opportunity, inclination, and intent must be proved.

2. *Desertion or Abandonment.* This must be continuous for a specified period of time. For example, if your husband deserts you in September and pops in to wish you a "Merry Christmas" in December, he has negated the ground of desertion.

Legally, desertion can also mean refusal to have intercourse. It can also signify being forcibly incarcerated in a prison or asylum.

The court accepts desertion as a ground when four things are present: no cohabitation, proof of the deserter's intent to stay away, absence of the other party's consent, and absence of any justified reason for deserting.

3. *Cruel and Inhuman Treatment.* Two or more witnesses must testify to physical violence, and it usually must be considered severe enough to endanger health or life and make living together unsafe. Mental cruelty is more difficult to prove, and it must be shown that it is more than temperamental incompatibility. (Some states now call this "conduct detrimental to the marriage.")

4. *Nonsupport.* If a husband is physically and mentally capable of earning a living and has refused to contribute to his family's economic needs, he can be sued for nonsupport.

5. *Habitual Drunkenness.* In some states this must persist over a period of one or two years.

6. *Insanity.* The condition must endure over a certain

period of time before the spouse can be adjudged insane.

7. *Impotency.* The mate must be found to be physically incapable of performing the sex act.

If you feel that one of these grounds can be proven to exist in your marriage relationship, your attorney can proceed to prepare your complaint. However, before so doing, he should suggest alternatives to divorce for your consideration. The most common are listed below.

Alternatives to Divorce

1. *Annulment.* A marriage can be annulled if at the time of the ceremony there was some defect, impediment, condition, or lack of capacity that prevented the marriage from being legal. These might include forcing marriage by pretending pregnancy, never intending to have intercourse in marriage, and being legally insane at the time of marriage. When a marriage is annulled, the court states that there never was a valid marriage, and the ex-wife resumes the use of her maiden name.

2. *Separate Maintenance.* This may be awarded to a wife who has committed no marital misbehavior and is living separate and apart from her husband. To receive this award, a wife must prove that she cannot bear living with her husband but that she needs the income from him in order to survive. She must also prove specifically what his misdeeds were and when they occurred.

3. *Legal separation.* This does not dissolve a marriage, but it does prohibit the marital partners from living together. The wife is entitled to support from her husband, and he may live apart from her without being considered guilty of desertion. However, they are still considered married in the eyes of the law, and neither may become involved sexually with another person, or marry a third person. The married partners are allowed to resume marital relations if they file a written statement of their desire with the clerk of the superior court in the county where their separation was processed.

4. *Criminal proceedings.* Another way to get a quick separation is to lodge a criminal complaint against your husband. If you can prove you have taken physical abuse from him, the court will put him in jail. The trouble with this procedure is that it may aggravate rather than solve your problems. The resulting bitterness and hostility and the fact that your mate can't earn any support money while in jail make such an action of dubious value.

The Mechanics of Divorce

If you have talked these alternatives over with your attorney and decided to go ahead with divorce, he will set the mechanics in motion.

First, he will have the divorce papers served to your husband, who has a specified period of time in which to reply or enter a countersuit. If he does not reply within that time, you can get a divorce by default. The same thing can happen to you if your husband is the plaintiff in the case. Recently a wife ignored divorce papers served to her because her husband told her someone must have sent them to her by mistake.. After the time for her replying had elapsed, her false sense of serenity was shattered when her husband bade her good-bye one day and never returned, and she was notified that he had been awarded a divorce. She had been left with no property settlement and no alimony and was legally helpless to do anything about it.

Second, the case will be entered on the court's calendar. If the court is a family court, a preliminary hearing will be scheduled before a referee, and after the hearing, if he thinks it advisable, he may refer you both for marriage counseling to see if reconciliation can be effected and divorce avoided.

There may also be an additional hearing scheduled to grant you temporary support until your case comes up on the court calendar.

Now, what might your husband be doing in the meantime? Even if he knows he is guilty of violating the marital code and realizes that you have enough evidence to prove your case, there are other steps he might take to prevent the divorce. He has the possibility of choosing one of these defenses.

Defenses Against Divorce

1. *Condonation.* If he can prove you have forgiven him by sleeping with him after you have learned that he has had an affair with another woman, his defense may be condonation. Incidentally, once you start the mechanics of divorce going, you dare not sleep with your husband. If you do, it quiets the action and your attorney must start a new suit.

2. *Connivance.* This means that your husband has information that you framed him by setting up evidence and witnesses that would help you obtain a divorce.

3. *Collusion.* This may be used if it can be shown that both conspired to create the necessary evidence for a divorce.

4. *Recrimination.* In most states, a fundamental part of divorce law holds that if both parties are at fault, neither one will be granted a divorce. For example, if you are suing your husband on the ground of adultery and he can prove that you also have been unfaithful, a divorce will not be granted.

5. *Countersuit.* If your husband does not want a divorce and none of the above conditions is present, he may still contest the divorce action by proving you guilty of a violation of the marital code.

Your Day in Court

If you have had helpful predivorce counseling, you and your husband have agreed on divorce terms, and he has decided not to contest your complaint, your day in court can be a relatively smooth, unemotional experience. The judge will read your attorney's written brief of complaints. Two or more witnesses will be called upon to testify that your complaints are valid, and the judge, if satisfied with your claims, can grant a divorce within a few minutes.

However, if your husband brings a countersuit to contest the divorce, watch out! Your case may drag on for days, months, or years, and by the time it is concluded, you may feel drained emotionally. The husband of one couple in a contested divorce case who came to me for predivorce counseling contacted me three years after court proceedings had started and stated that legal costs had reached $16,000 with still no settlement in sight.

When the divorce hearing is concluded, the judge will hand down certain decisions that will affect you, your husband, and your children for years to come.

If the opposing attorneys have not worked out pre-court agreements, the *division of property* may pose many problems. In most settlements, the wife receives one-third to one-half of the property. However, irrational statements by either spouse such as, "Wow, will I make that rat pay," or "I won't give her one penny without a fight," can lead to confusion. And the court will be forced to resolve such specific issues as who gets the family car, who should keep the dog, who gets the best bed, and so forth.

The amount of *alimony* awarded is determined by several factors, such as the wife's needs as related to her accustomed standard of living, the husband's ability to pay, and in some cases the degree of moral misconduct on the part of either the husband or wife. A court order is issued directing the husband to pay a specified amount until the ex-wife dies or remarries. In some cases, even if the wife remarries, she may still collect alimony if her second spouse cannot support her "in the manner and station of the first husband."

The usual amount of alimony awarded is one-quarter or one-third of the husband's income. A husband can be forced to pay alimony by having the court attach his salary or property or put him in jail.

The *custody of the children* is usually decided on the

basis of what best serves the interests of the child. Although judges may differ in their evaluation of specific circumstances, several guiding principles are followed in awarding custody.

1. Mothers are generally favored in custody disputes, particularly if the children are very young.

2. The parent who is not at fault in the divorce action is usually given custody.

3. The child's preference for one parent may affect but will not determine the custody award.

4. The parents' rights to custody of the children are superior to those of relatives.

5. Courts are reluctant to permit the spouse who has custody to move the children out of state.

6. The parent who is considered unfit to bring up a child may be denied custody.

7. Unless it is proven detrimental to the child's welfare, the court will insist that the parent deprived of custody have visitation rights.

As long as he is able to do so, the husband is required to support the children until they reach legal age. In setting the amount to pay, the court decides according to the father's ability to pay and the needs of the child.

You must realize that the foregoing brief summary of divorce procedures can do no more than make you aware of some of the problems you must face if you consider divorce. Additional details and precise information concerning your specific situation must come from your attorney. Nevertheless, a careful consideration of the information given here should enable you to deal in a more confident manner with your contemplated divorce.

Summary

If you are considering a divorce, remember:
The grass on the other side of the fence may look greener than it is.

You will probably exchange a life you are acquainted with for the unknown.

Divorce is expensive, both financially and emotionally.

You have no assurance that you will be happier after.

5

After Divorce, What?

"I had fasted and prayed about it and felt that separation was the only way out. The actual divorce took less time than my marriage ceremony, and in a few brief moments my life was completely changed. I was facing the world alone with responsibilities that seemed too heavy to bear."

As you walk out of the divorce court, you will take your first steps into a new life. It will help your mental health if you are already visualizing interesting future plans.

You can hardly expect to be as joyful as one divorcee who said, "What a relief! Now that I'm rid of him, I'm free for the first time in years to do what I really want."

Neither will it be helpful to be as depressed as the woman who said, "Now I'm alone, I feel that my life is empty. I might as well be dead."

A sounder attitude than either of the above was expressed by a nationally known woman who has dedicated her post-divorce life to helping others.

"Divorce meant a rebirth to me," she said. "I have

learned that one must give of oneself. There is no substitute for personal involvement in helping others. It can become one of the most exciting, stimulating, and rewarding things in life. There is too much to be done to experience an idle moment. When a woman has a great upheaval, she can either rush into the arms of the first available man and think that it will solve all her loneliness and strife, or she can evaluate the demands on her at the moment."[1]

The above thoughts and those that follow have been given here to assist you in thinking about your future plans and see if we can help make your transition from married to single life easier.

In the first place, try not to be too hard on yourself. You can't expect to bounce back like a rubber ball. Strange as it may seem, society does put this kind of pressure on divorced people. It is taken for granted that an individual who has undergone surgery will need a period for recovery in a hospital and a planned convalescence afterward. But a woman or man who has undergone the emotional upheaval of divorce is expected to immediately resume her or his normal routines. There may also be some negative feelings toward you. One divorcee put it this way, "Why is it that society looks upon a widow with pity and empathy and upon a divorcee with disgust, when both have gone through a crisis?"

It can be difficult to establish a new pattern of day-to-day living within the framework of providing for emotional, economic, and social needs. For example, one divorcee said, "I was so used to setting a place at the breakfast table for my husband that I still find myself putting dishes and utensils at the place where he used to sit. And if I get a flat tire, my first impulse is to get my husband to fix it, and then I suddenly realize he isn't available."

Your friends and associates are not always sensitive to these things that are going on behind the scenes in your

---

[1]Mrs. Eleanor Whitney (the former Mrs. Cornelius Vanderbilt Whitney), *New York Times Service*, February 7, 1972.

life, and it is much better to talk to an understanding counselor about them than to bottle up your feelings or face your problems alone.

The degree of your emotional attachment to your ex-husband may also have a bearing on your ability to adjust. Studies by William J. Goode show that about one-fourth of divorced women who have a high intensity contact with their former spouses (date them, see them, know what they are doing, do not avoid seeing them) feel that they still love them.

On the other hand, such contact causes some divorcees to reinforce their basic feelings that their ex-husband is a wrong-doer who should be punished.

Still other women feel guilty about their divorce and begin to think it was mostly their fault.

One of the best ways to regain peace of mind after an emotional upset such as that caused by a divorce is to talk frequently with our Heavenly Father. He is always available to strengthen one's spirit. As one woman said, "I can always talk to God and know that he will not misunderstand, misinterpret, or tell others the things that I confide in him."

Prayer, in addition to giving spiritual strength, also helps psychologically. Our one-to-one relationship with God will reinforce the knowledge that we are children of God and have special roles to play in life. Consequently, it is easier to view one's single status as an opportunity for continued growth and development. We all need to realize that each day provides opportunities to learn something new, to be of service, and to make new friends. This helps calm our emotions because we remember that the purpose of life still stays the same whether we are married or single.

Making Living Adjustments

If your husband has been awarded rights of visitation with the children, do your best to make these contacts satisfying. One divorcee said she cringed every time she knew her husband was scheduled to visit the children. And she finally became so emotionally upset thinking about his coming that she would get her children dressed and ready to go out. Then she would push them outside the front door so he could pick them up without crossing her threshhold.

Such behavior heightens tension in the situation. It is much better to relax and accept your ex-spouse's visits to your children as part of the family's schedule.

However, such an attitude is based on the assumption that your husband's behavior is appropriate to the situation. If his manner is such that he attempts to harass or intimidate you or the children, you will be justified in returning to court to ask that his visits be modified or terminated.

Women who are divorced say that they have to handle their money very carefully. Even though you have been awarded alimony and child support, your budget will be cut. This is so because your ex-husband's salary will now be divided to maintain two separate household units.

If your children are small and you need additional income, you will be faced with planning how to earn it. Even if you have a job skill, there are decisions to be made regarding care of your children, such as selecting a day nursery or hiring a live-in babysitter.

If you have no previous job experience or skill to offer, you might want to consider training or further schooling. Don't hesitate to call upon your bishop or the Church Social Services for counsel. If such is not available, good places to contact are local Community Chest and the Family and Children's Service Societies in your town.

Inasmuch as the Church has its own welfare program, provision for your additional financial needs can be arranged for within its framework. However, if for some reason you don't qualify for Church assistance, your county welfare department stands ready to offer help with its Aid for Families with Dependent Children arrangement or with some other program.

One young divorced mother praised the personnel of her welfare department. She said, "I found that I had falsely stereotyped welfare workers as having a negative attitude toward anyone who needed their services. Those who helped me really cared. In addition, they were logical and loving."

The point to remember in making economic adjustments is that there are many people who are ready to lend a helping hand. Don't hesitate to contact them. This will not only benefit you but also those who help you.

Social Adjustments

Some divorced women contend that they feel like a fifth wheel when they try to resume contacts with their former social circle.

Typical of these was Mary A., who said, "All the members of my former social group are couples, and now that I am single, I no longer seem to fit in. I have the feeling that some of the women consider me a possible threat to their marriage, especially if their husbands are friendly to me. Others treat me in a patronizing manner and seem uncomfortable when I am around."

This should not happen in Church social circles, but if it does, it is simply another indication that Church members are also human. One reason that it might happen is that married and single people do not always have the same interests and often find that their conversations become awkward and strained. Church leaders are aware of these problems in social interaction, and consequently, have set up the Special Interests program to provide social activities for all those single individuals who are over twenty-six years of age. Some of the stimulating things offered in this program as well as in others outside of the Church will be discussed in a later chapter.

Perhaps the best procedure to follow in resuming

social activities is to move slowly until you learn in which groups you feel comfortable and accepted.

Of course, your own attitude will have much to do with the development of a satisfying social life.

One thing that might affect your social attitudes is how you feel about wearing your rings. One woman asked, "Now that I am divorced, should I discard my wedding and engagement rings?"

There is no clear-cut answer to this question. It all depends upon how you feel about them. Some divorcees at Reno, Nevada, celebrate a so-called "graduation day" and throw their rings into a wishing well. Such a ceremony would only be for the callously unsentimental.

If you have growing children and want to preserve a family feeling for them, you will probably decide to leave both of your rings right on the third finger of your left hand without giving the matter a second thought. Some wives follow a different pattern and shift them to other fingers or have them reset. Naturally, it's your decision to make. You know best how you feel about wearing them, so don't let what anyone else thinks bother you.

Our friends enjoy our company more if we avoid talking about unpleasant experiences. For example, we all shy away from the individual who repeatedly recounts the details of his or her latest operation.

When we are tempted to talk about our problems, it is better to dwell on the good things that have happened to us. Repeating a divorce story not only upsets the individual but can also bore listeners who have heard it before. It is better for all of us to close the book on the past and get our minds on pleasant things.

Openly criticizing your ex-husband and blaming him may cause hostility between you and lessen your chances of reconciliation. It may also discourage other men from dating you, as they may falsely assume you are a "man-hater." And it may make your children turn against him and feel the insecurity of having no male image to identify with.

Blaming your in-laws for the divorce may also cause strained or severed relations between your children and their relatives and make other people wonder if you are hard to get along with.

Continually thinking about your divorce may make you miserable and unhappy and cause miserable and unhappy people to gravitate toward you.

The best way to stop talking about your divorce is to get your mind on other things. How?

You can observe interesting things around you, react to what is going on in today's world, read good books, become involved in activities that require meeting with people, or accept a church job and give your best efforts to it.

Making New Friends

Divorce does not necessarily mean "off with the old and on with the new," as far as friends are concerned. But it may cause changes by extending or narrowing one's circle of friends. It could provide a testing of the sincerity of old friends, and divorced people often find that some will stay with them and others will not.

You may also have opportunities to make new friends if you take a job, move to a different locality, or join church groups or clubs that are composed of single, divorced, and widowed women.

When associating with new people, we should try to avoid wearing our feelings on our sleeve and refrain from talking about our own troubles. One way to do this is to get interested in these individuals and learn about their varied activities and attitudes. Detailed information about organizations a divorced woman may join is given in chapter 13.

Dating

Pat B. said, "It took me a while after my divorce to get in the mood for dating. But when I started, I was surprised to learn that most of my dates expected me to go to bed with them. Their argument was, 'You've been married and know the score. Your body will function better if you have sexual intercourse, and after all, we're not a couple of high school kids, so why waste time with preliminaries?'

"These men all turned me off, and I will stay home rather than date men with such standards."

Mary A., who has been married twice and has four children, has reacted differently to male dating advances. She rather defiantly stated that she does not particularly care how old her date is, or how he looks; she makes it very clear that she's willing to have sex with him. Many times she plays the role of the aggressor. All the man has to do is find a place and be there. Her sex relationships are very short and limited to chance meetings, and she doesn't care who knows about them.

It is apparent that both Pat and Mary have a problem. Pat's is to find a man with high moral standards like her own, while Mary's is to refind herself and realize that her present behavior is destroying her womanhood.

Now, what about you? If you confine your dating to a good, faithful Latter-day Saint man, this problem of resisting or giving in to sexual advances should not come up. However, even if you both are active Church members, you are also both human, and loneliness may drive you into each other's arms with overemphasis on physical affection even though neither intends it.

Consequently, it is wise to be as objective as possible when you start dating again and to avoid rushing into a relationship because you hunger for a mate.

We are sure that your thinking will be, "This time it will be forever," and you will weigh the pleasures of the moment against the rewards of a satisfying eternal relationship.

Summary

First adjustments to divorce are not easy. It helps to—

 —seek spiritual help as a child of God who has a special role to play in life.
 —quit talking about divorce.
 —face economic problems with realism.
 —keep active spiritually and socially.
 —date with thoughts extending beyond today into eternity.
 —keep involved in things outside of one's self.

PART FOUR

Those who have
never married

6

Single by Choice

There are a number of reasons why individuals remain single.

Some choose the single state because they feel they can serve more people. Typical of these are persons who elect to work in educational or social service fields. They feel that people of all ages are part of their family and they can serve them more effectively if they remain unmarried.

Such an attitude was demonstrated by a woman who was a vice-principal of a high school. Miss B., as she was affectionately called by her students, was a source of encouragement to everyone who came into her office. She was firm but kind, and although she worked with a male principal who outranked her, it was quite evident that she was the one who kept the school functioning efficiently. Her concern for the students in her charge was so deep that she contributed financially for some of them to go on to college. And many students were proud to be known as part of Miss B.'s family.

There are other reasons why many women choose

to follow careers instead of marrying. One is accounted for by the great opportunities afforded them in the world of work.

Pearl S. Buck, noted author, says in *American Women: The Changing Image* that never before in history has a woman, especially in America, enjoyed such equal opportunity with men for education and taking jobs in the workaday world. She continues, "To educate her for mobility and freedom and then deny her that same mobility and freedom can only lead to frustration, and a frustrated woman is not a good wife and mother."

Of course, many women solve this problem by combining a career with marriage, and say that they feel absolutely no sense of frustration as wives and mothers. And then there are homemakers who feel that being good companions to their husbands and rearing their children properly constitute the greatest challenge of their lives, and that pursuing a career is of minor importance.

On the other hand, a woman who finds that her career completely absorbs her time and says, "Being single makes it possible to devote more time effectively to my work," may have little interest in getting married.

A few individuals forgo marriage because they have been parted by death, or some other circumstance, from one they love. This was true of Helen M.

Helen is competent in her job, attractive, and popular. Several years ago she was happily engaged and preparing for her wedding. At that time her fiancé was unexpectedly offered a high-salaried position overseas. He took the job, and they parted with the understanding that he would send for her in two weeks and make her his bride.

Several years have gone by and Helen has not heard one word from her husband-to-be. Today she says, "Little did I realize that he was flying out of my life forever. He is either married to someone else, living alone, or dead. How can I even think of letting myself be affectionate with any other man? In fact, I don't think I could even trust one."

Like Helen, many of us suffer disillusioning experiences as we go through life, but we usually fare better if we can put them behind us. Remembering that a disappointing experience with one person will not necessarily be repeated with another may prevent us from overlooking a possible mate who might bring all we desire to a marriage relationship.

A large number of women and men do not marry because of duties to dependents. Some take care of younger brothers and sisters. Others support aged and infirm parents. Such a sense of loyalty may cause an individual to remain at home and pass up opportunities for marriage until the chances of finding a suitable mate diminish.

Overpossessive parents often foster such a tie. This happened to Pamela. She turned down three marriage proposals because she felt it was her duty to live with her ailing mother. This was done despite the fact that she had a married brother and two married sisters who could have had their mother stay with them.

Pamela died without marrying, and her surviving mother subsequently went to live with one of Pamela's married sisters.

An unhappy home life in which conflict between parents has caused a single person to look upon marriage as a risky venture causes some to remain single.

Others may feel that the sex act in marriage is a distasteful activity. This often develops as a result of learning the story of human procreation in an undignified context.

The right man has not yet come along is given by over one-half of single women as a reason for forgoing marriage. This reason bears some discussion.

Surely a mature woman will prefer to remain single than to attempt an unwise marriage. However, some single women reveal that the criteria they have used in determining if a man is the right one have been too high. Such an attitude is frequently contributed to by parents who demand too much in a mate for their children and feel that no one is good enough for them. Because of these high expectations, it occasionally happens, as one single woman said, that "the right man came along but married someone else."

If a single woman says that she has not married because the right man has not come along, and then adds that she has aimed too high in choosing a companion, it might be wisdom for her to settle for less and quit seeking a man who is a combination of a Fred Astaire on the dance floor, a J. Paul Getty in the business world, and a David O. McKay in the home.

Of course, this is an exaggerated example of demanding outstanding characteristics in a future mate, but it might serve to illustrate the point that people who marry should come as close as they can to their ideal mate and not expect perfection.

After reviewing the reasons individuals give for not marrying, it is apparent that the decision to remain single is related to one's temperament and the life-style one wishes to pursue. The important thing to remember is that married or single, all of us will lead more satisfying lives if we retain enthusiasm for life, try to enjoy people, and link ourselves to great causes.

Summary

Those who don't marry have many sound reasons for remaining single.

Temperament and desired life-style combined with the wish to serve mankind in a certain manner play important parts in deciding whether to marry.

Whether we are single or married our lives will be more satisfying if we—
—retain enthusiasm for life,
—try to enjoy people,
—link ourselves to a great cause.

7

Decisions Facing
the Unwed Mother

Heather came into my office, sat down, and said, in a voice trembling with emotion, "I have a problem that you must help me with."

"I'll try," I replied. "Are you having trouble with your grades?"

"I wish it were no worse than that," she said; then, bursting into tears, she stammered, "I—I'm two months pregnant and I don't know what to do. Promise me you won't tell a soul. I just couldn't bear to have people find out."

"Don't your parents know?" I asked.

"My parents?" Heather shuddered. "They'd disown me if they ever found out."

Heather's thinking illustrates the feelings of a large number of single girls who become pregnant. They want to keep it a secret, and they don't know where to turn for help.

Incidentally, Heather was encouraged to tell her parents, which she did, and after talking it over with them, she reported, "My parents were just wonderful. I could tell they were upset, but they told me how much they love me, and they are doing everything possible to help me. I should have known I could count on them."

If you are in the same situation as Heather, single and pregnant, you undoubtedly feel the need to have someone offer you sympathetic understanding and help you with your immediate concrete problems. Let's look at the first problem, that of telling others that you are pregnant.

First, whom should you tell? If you live with your parents, or if you do not and they can be contacted, it would be wise to talk it over with them. As a counselor, I have discovered that the majority of parents rally around their pregnant daughters and do all they can to help. Of course, if you feel that your relationships with your parents are impossible because your family has been torn apart by divorce, or because of other factors, then you have an individual decision to make.

Should you tell your boyfriend? It seems rather strange to even ask this question, but it is given here because of the way some pregnant girls think. Such statements as the following have been heard during counseling sessions:

"I don't love him anymore. Why should I tell him he got me pregnant?"

"I'm too proud to tell him. He'd shoot me down and say I was careless or I wouldn't be in this fix."

"He'd go all to pieces and just couldn't face the responsibility."

Of course, you know best what your boyfriend's personality is and what kind of relationship you have with him. But you must have had some sense of commitment to each other to be sexually intimate, so you should surely know each other well enough to discuss your pregnancy. Such a discussion might also cause him to realize more clearly the decisions that lie ahead for you, and he then can contribute his insights to help you make the best ones.

In addition to telling your parents and your boyfriend about your pregnancy, in either order you deem advisable, you should also inform someone who is in a position to counsel or arrange for counseling. If you are a member of The Church of Jesus Christ of Latter-day Saints and live in an area where there is a bishop or branch president, it would be wise to contact him. He will be glad to help and, if you desire, will also refer you to the Church Social Services. If you are a Church member in an area where such help is not available, your local Community Chest organizations, social service agencies, university, or county welfare department will offer assistance.

If you are not a member of the Church, you can get help from your minister or the other sources previously mentioned.

What Should You Do Next?

After you have told those with whom you want to share knowledge of your pregnancy, your next step is to make an appointment to see a doctor. This can be done with family or church help. If such help is not available, the organizations already mentioned can direct you to an understanding doctor or, if necessary, a free clinic. The doctor will examine you, check your physical condition carefully, suggest proper diet and exercises, and tell you the approximate date that you can expect to deliver your baby.

As soon as seeing a doctor is mentioned, some girls want to know if it would be possible to terminate the pregnancy with an induced abortion. Today, pro-abortionists are suggesting that a pregnant woman should have the sole right to decide about terminating a pregnancy. The law previously stated that two or more doctors had to agree that continuing your pregnancy would endanger your life or cause a breakdown of your physical or mental health, before a legal (therapeutic) abortion might be performed.

However, the U.S. Supreme Court's recent decision has made abortion legal during the first six months of pregnancy and has also left the decision to have an abortion up to the woman and her personal physician. This has stirred up much controversy, but should in no way affect the attitude of the individual who regards human life as sacred.

Naturally, if you are a religious person, you will banish the thought of anything but a therapeutic abortion because you know that you would be deliberately destroying life and depriving one of God's children of the right to a body.

If you have no religious belief and are considering an abortion, you should still ask yourself:

Will I constantly wonder about how life would have been with my baby?

Will I later want a baby when I am married and not be able to have one?

Will I finally realize that I am a child of God and have acted contrary to his purposes?

Should you get married because of pregnancy?

This is a question that has no set answer. One way to approach it is to ask yourself if you and your boyfriend are getting married primarily because of your pregnancy. If this is the only reason, there are grave doubts that your marriage will succeed. The chances are that your hurried-up marriage may find you both unready to accept domestic responsibilities and unwilling to settle down with one person. A feeling of being trapped into marriage and tied to a partner you don't enjoy may cause either or both of you to rebel and your relationship to deteriorate.

Take Betty's case as an illustration. When Betty became pregnant, she and both sets of parents insisted that Dick marry her, which he did, producing disastrous results.

She said, "Dick and I soon found that we're completely unsuited to each other. We keep getting into arguments, and our life together is one of constant tension and emotional strain. I know I'm partly at fault

because I'm always nagging, but Dick is completely ir-
responsible. He can't keep a job, wants to chase around
every night with the boys, and treats me like a piece of
household furniture. I don't know what I ever saw in him.
I suppose I gave myself to him sexually beause I thought
it would be a romantic adventure. Now I can't even get
Dick to go to church, and as far as I'm concerned, life
holds no meaning. I'm hanging on to our marriage for
our baby's sake, but I can't take it much longer."

To look at the other side of the picture, it should be
stated, however, that sometimes couples who marry when
the girl is pregnant do work things out satisfactorily.
The generalization might be made that this happens because both people are genuinely ready for marriage and
would have married each other anyway, even if pregnancy
had not occurred. Such a couple has undoubtedly developed a more complete relationship in which there is not
only mutual physical attraction, but also mental com-
patibility and spiritual harmony. The young man does not
see marriage as a threat to his educational or vocational
plans, and the young woman feels that the marriage will
not curtail her opportunities to grow as an individual and
develop her talents. In other words, both of the partners
feel that they will have greater oportunity to accomplish
their goals in marriage than they would have had as single
individuals.

Such was the case with Terry and Barbara, both college students. They came for counseling and help when
Barbara was in her sixth month of pregnancy.

Terry said, "I love Barbara dearly, and we want you
to help us arrange a quiet marriage out of town so when
we have our baby we can tell our friends that we have
been secretly married for a long time."

"Can you make a go of things financially?" I asked.

"Indeed we can," replied Barbara. "We are both
working part-time after school, and Terry will receive his
degree this spring, after which the company that he is
working for has promised him a good full-time job."

"You don't feel that you're being pressured to marry?" I asked, turning to Terry.

"By no means," said Terry. "We have been planning to marry for a long time. Of course, we know it would have been better if we hadn't gone all the way sexually and gotten Barbara pregnant, but the important thing to us now is to get married, have our baby, and begin living like we want to as a married couple."

So, after discussing how they would tell their families and considering a number of other things, Terry and Barbara got married. They paid me a visit several years later, both genuinely happy and eager to show me their little family of three children.

This example is given to point out that it is possible for marriage to work out satisfactorily when pregnancy has occurred while you are single. However, before you make a decision either way to marry or not to marry, you should discuss all the facets of your situation with your church leader or a trained counselor.

If you don't marry, where should you live during your pregnancy?

During the time that you are expecting your baby, you must still go on living. In order to avoid feelings of depression, your living conditions should be the best possible. If societal pressures make it difficult to live at home with your parents or in your hometown, there are other arrangements that might be made. Some girls visit a distant relative until the baby comes. Occasionally an older girl will get an apartment and, when the baby comes due, will deliver it under an assumed name at a nearby hospital. The last two choices are of dubious value in that one often burdens a relative with a problem that is too difficult to handle at home, and the other finds the new mother delivering her child in a hospital maternity wing without sharing with relatives and friends the joy of having a new baby.

A possible living arrangement that should be considered is living with and working for a nonrelative family during the period of pregnancy. The Church Social Services department and other agencies can place you in such a home with understanding people who have been carefully selected to help you.

The usually recommended living arrangement, if things cannot be worked out at home, is to go to a home for unmarried mothers in a large city. Again, a church counselor or a social worker can direct you to such a home. There you will be assured of good prenatal and delivery care and have your baby safely and in relative secrecy.

Such a home, if it is run properly, can transform your pregnancy from a dreary period of waiting to a positive and vital experience. You will have the opportunity to live in a warm, cheerful atmosphere. Adults who care will help you, and other pregnant girls will offer you companionship. In these homes, classes are taught in which high school credits may be earned, and if you are older and your school days are behind you, crafts and many other things may be learned. High school graduation exercises may be held there, and Christmas parties and other observances help speed the time.

Some criticism has been voiced regarding these homes for unmarried mothers, such as that there is too much regimentation and girls are often treated inhumanely. These thoughts may have arisen because girls who entered did not acquaint themselves with the policies of the home beforehand.

The writer spent several years as a part-time consultant and group therapist at one of the largest homes for unmarried mothers in the nation, and from personal experience can vouch for the fact that these homes are designed to offer invaluable help to the single, pregnant girl. If breakdowns in interpersonal relations occur, it is because of the human element—the temperament and personalities of staff members and the involved pregnant girls.

Finally, it should be said that no matter where you

live during your pregnancy, you should take advantage
of opportunities to learn and grow as a person. Your
pregnancy should not be looked upon as something that
will put an end to your life plans, but rather as an experience that will help you to understand life and its
purposes more fully.

What should you do with your baby?

According to studies, adoption gives both the mother
and the baby the opportunity for the best life chance in
the majority of cases. This is said to be so because, if the
adoptive parents have been carefully selected (which is the
social agency's responsibility), they are in a position to
give the baby the immediate opportunities and advantages
that it deserves. Such advantages would include love and
understanding, a stable home life, and the material things
necessary for proper growth and development.

If you, as a pregnant girl, follow the adoption procedure, you will also gain additional help in the form
of various services. Rehabilitative casework counseling is
available at your request; help is given in obtaining resi-
dential prenatal facilities; and in some areas funds are
made available to defray the expenses of your medical
care.

A final consideration is that if you, as the natural
mother, feel that you are not ready for the responsibilities
of motherhood and cannot face the burden of rearing an
out-of-wedlock child, placing your baby for adoption will
enable you to carry on your life as you had planned before
you became pregnant.

You must remember, however, when you place your
baby for adoption, that you must close the book on this
phase of your life, as there is little possibility that you will
ever know anything about your baby's future. However,
you can pretty safely assume that it will be well taken
care of.

The writer has been in a position to observe and
counsel many college students who have been adopted as
well as a number of adoptive parents, and in the majority

of cases, there has been a fine relationship between the adopted child and his parents.

In some cases, your parents or close relatives may welcome the opportunity to have a new baby in the home, either to take partial or full responsibility for it. It may lift their spirits, make up for the loss of another child, or compensate for other things that they lack to have a good family relationship.

Here are two ways in which such an arrangement seems to work out quite well: first, when you live with them, the baby is recognized as yours, and the entire family shares the joys and the responsibilities that the tiny newcomer brings, and second, when your parents and relatives agree and are happy to care for the baby until you are in a position to support it financially or get married and want the child to live with you and your husband. In neither case would you relinquish your rights as a mother.

Giving your baby to parents or relatives is a completely different matter. Trouble does occur sometimes when a pregnant girl gives her baby outright to her parents or relatives and gives up her identity as its mother. This should never be done without weighing the present carefully against the future. Before you consider such a step, try to envision what your future life would be living with such an arrangement.

Joan was considering such a decision, but after she weighed the present against the future she said, "My parents insist that I give them my baby. Oh, I know they can give it everything—a comfortable home, a good education, and opportunities to meet nice people. But I simply can't do it. It would tear me apart to be on the sidelines watching my baby grow up, without ever being allowed to divulge that I was her mother.

"I hope to get married some day, and I want to be able to tell my husband about my child. If he loves children and wants her in our home, it would be unfair to him not to have her and it would be unfair to my parents to take her away from them. I can't do it."

Should you keep your baby and bring it up yourself?

You must be realistic about considering this decision. Rearing your child alone as an unmarried mother is a heavy responsibility, no matter where you live. The chances are that you will have to work in order to support your child and yourself. And even if you receive welfare help and can place your child in a day-care center while you work, there still will be other things to consider. Will you have sufficient energy to work, care for your child, and, if you desire, continue your schooling on a part-time basis? If you are at the age in life when you would normally be out having fun with other girls and dating young men, will you resent staying home alone with your baby night after night? Will you gradually look upon your child as a burden rather than a joy?

Natalie, an attractive college student, touched on some of these problems when she said, "I do love my little Mary, who is eight, but bringing her up by myself hasn't been easy. The first thing new friends ask is, 'What happened to your husband?' If I tell them the truth, some of them treat me like a streetwalker. And, if I hide the facts, I live in a constant state of tension, fearing that someone else may tell them what happened.

"In social groups, I feel like a 'fifth wheel.' I just don't seem to belong. Married women view me as a threat. And men! The married ones act like they are afraid to be friendly, and the single ones want to go to bed with me. If I didn't have my school studies to concentrate on, I'd be climbing the walls. I really feel as if life is passing me by because I just don't seem to belong anywhere."

Karen's story, told by another unwed mother, illustrates how the joy of bearing a child can be tempered by the realities of adjusting to a life that requires self-discipline and emotional stability. She said:

"I had a beautiful, healthy, blonde-haired baby girl, 7 pounds $3\frac{1}{2}$ ounces, born on July 11, 1970, at 6:34 A.M. What an experience! The most beautiful thing that has ever happened to me in my whole life was giving birth!

"Now that Amy was born, I had to face the big decision that I had been pondering over for nine months. Should I keep her? I had made up my mind several times and then, after doing some heavy thinking, changed it.

"There were many factors to consider such as: Am I ready and mature enough to settle down and raise a child? What is fair to the child? And what is fair to myself? Decisions, decisions, if only there were not so many decisions to be made in life!

"After deciding to keep Amy, I found an apartment that I liked and immediately rented. I was also eligible for AFDC, as I had applied for it and had been accepted as soon as I got out of the hospital. My only reason for going on welfare was because I couldn't possibly make enough money on my own to suport the two of us. Being a very ambitious person and going to school brings about my main goal of wanting to be self-supporting. So, after getting an apartment, Amy and I lived there for nine months and then moved to a small two-bedroom house in Hillsdale, where we now live.

"Now for some of the negative feelings I have toward society. When you are pregnant out of wedlock, you constantly feel the icy stares from people and the looking down at your hand to find a wedding ring. Perhaps some of this perception was a guilt feeling on my part, but I'm not sure I'll ever really admit it. It is certainly hard when you are somewhere with your child and someone admiringly says, 'She sure is adorable. I bet your husband really loves her.' That was a true experience, hard to accept, but one of those things you learn to take in stride.

"My feelings made me gradually withdraw into my own little world for a time. After beginning housekeeping, I didn't have the desire to really see anyone but my family and very close friends. I did come out of my shell a little but not completely. I was, so to speak, hiding under a rock for about a year. I am now starting to come out of my cocoon and am experiencing a rebirth. Being a broad-minded person, I realize that not all in life is disappointing. I know there is some good in this world, and I'm bound and determined to find it out!

"We are getting along fine, but life is not 'a bowl of cherries.' It is very hard for a mother to raise a child by herself. The hardest part of it for me is the total mental responsibility; by this I mean not being able to share any mental responsibility with a mate. But I do *love* being a mother, and Amy is the sunshine in my life. She is now a year and a half old."

After reviewing the decisions to consider and eventually make, I am sure that you will agree that there are no easy solutions to unwed motherhood. And no matter what decision you make, there may be unhappy results you will have to live with.

However, the thing to always keep in mind is that you and your baby are both children of God, and that with sufficient faith and the willingness to discuss and work on the problems in your situation, you will be led to the decision that is best for both of you. There are many concerned and understanding people who stand ready to help you.

Summary

Only God has control over human life.

A successful marriage must be built on a much broader base than a premarital pregnancy.

Studies show that placing a baby for adoption gives a mother and her baby the opportunity for the best life chance in the majority of cases.

The joy derived from keeping a baby may be offset by future circumstances that are hard to endure.

Each child is one of God's spirits and should be afforded the best life possible.

Keeping your baby may provide you with the incentive to grow as a person, if you are mature enough to accept all of the responsibilities.

No decision regarding the baby's future should be made before seeking wise counsel.

8

For Those Who
Would Like to Marry

Judy S., a single girl in her late thirties who has never
married, shifted uneasily in her chair, lowered her blonde
head, and tried vainly to hold back the tears as she told
her story.

"I have always gone to church, but two years ago the
bottom seemed to drop out of things, so I went for special
counseling. I was searching for a sense of meaning in my
life and I couldn't find it."

"Meaning?" I asked. "Doesn't church activity help
you find it?"

"Not really," she said as her pretty face became
flushed with emotion. "Of course, I know we're here to
strive for eternal exaltation, but I need a man to help me.
I just can't do it by myself. I need meaning in my life
now."

"You've wanted to get married for a long time, then?"

"Desperately! But it has never happened. I can't
understand why."

"Tell me a little about yourself," I said.

"Well, my parents were unhappy. My mother was always bored or sick or something. And when I was young, I guess they kind of turned me off toward marriage. Nevertheless, they were good to me and helped me through college. I was a good student, but all during my school days I was so shy I couldn't relate to boys. And my parents didn't help matters either. They worked until midnight every day fixing up their rental property and left me to take care of my younger brother and sister. If I did have a date, my mother made me clean the house before I could go out, and she always acted upset when I was away.

"In my associations with boys, I didn't know what to say or do. When fellows tried to be affectionate with me, I couldn't stand it. And if they wanted to sleep with me, I dropped them flat. I'm glad I held to these standards, but still I wasn't even aware of sex and didn't understand that it has a special place in a happy marriage.

"So, I guess I compensated for not having a male companion by striving for professional achievements. I taught school, served for a time as an officer in the woman's branch of the army, and traveled widely. Finally everything seemed meaningless, and as I said before, I went to a professional counselor."

"Did he help?"

"Help?" Judy blushed. "Frankly, he made things worse. He immediately asked about my sex life, and when I told him there wasn't any, he suggested that I relieve my sexual tensions by stimulating myself. When I said I didn't know how, he explained the technique. This was so repugnant to me that I never went back to him. But his instructions had made me aware that I had a sexual body. Consequently, I found myself reading books on sex and going swimming a lot to work off my sex needs. I still couldn't be affectionate with fellows, and one accused me of being a Lesbian."

"I assume that you have never found a fellow with whom you feel comfortable?"

Judy hesitated, and then with some reluctance she said, "I finally have. That's why I've come to you for advice."

"I'll try to help," I replied.

"Well, Brent's 44 and the most wonderful and understanding man I've ever met. He's everything I've ever wanted. I can talk to him freely about anything that's on my mind, and best of all, he doesn't scare me sexually. In fact, I want to be affectionate with him."

"So, you want help in controlling your sex desires until you get married. Is that the problem?"

"I guess it could be one of them, but the big one is that he's already married."

"Married?"

"Yes. With a wife and four children—two married and two still at home."

"Does he want to get a divorce and marry you?"

"No, he doesn't. He says he has a responsibility to his wife and children. But his wife is physically indifferent to him, and he has a tremendous need for warmth, tenderness, and physical affection that only I can give him."

"Let me get this straight. He wants you to be his mistress. Right?

"Right."

"How will his wife react to this?"

"She'll never know. They live in another city a thousand miles away, so he can stay with me on his business trips here and no one will be the wiser. Dr. Anderson, tell me it's all right. I'm 38 years old and have never had sexual intercourse. It may be my last chance. After all, I'm human and I have a body that needs loving. He's coming to town this weekend and wants to go to bed with me, and I want just as much to go to bed with him. Is it so wrong for a woman my age to become one physically with a man she loves?"

"Judy," I said, "you're asking me to make a decision that only you can make. Let's discuss your feelings and see if the consummation of your physical love for Brent will give the meaning to life that you have been seeking."

So we discussed at length the pros and cons of Judy's becoming Brent's mistress. She seemed to be considering the situation objectively, and when she left, she promised to phone and tell me how she handled the weekend with Brent.

Did Judy become Brent's mistress? I can't tell you. I have never heard from her since our interview.

Judy's counseling interview has been given here to point out several factors that seem to be present in the lives of some girls who have not married. Like Judy, they have spent their childhood with unhappy parents, have had no sound teaching about human sexuality, have not been taught how to communicate or develop social skills, and have often looked upon men as threats rather than satisfying companions. Then, after years of frustration, they have become fair game for "misunderstood married men" who want to enjoy their beautiful bodies without making any commitment to them.

If some of these things ring a bell in your memory, or you, at present, are faced with a situation similar to Judy's, there are three helpful things you can do.

1. Remember, it doesn't help us to brood over the past.

If we had an unhappy childhood and never developed the self-confidence to interact comfortably and happily with the opposite sex, we should try not to think about it. Worrying about the past can be as futile as trying to piece together a mirror that has been shattered into a thousand bits and pieces.

2. Select the things from this list that might have prevented you from marrying and see if you can do something about them.

    a. Ill health
    b. Pessimistic outlook
    c. Family obligations

    d. Wrong job (try to get one where you can meet more eligible men)

    e. Anxieties about responsibilities of marriage and parenthood

    f. Seeing a man as a threat to personal independence

    g. Financial pressures

    h. Lack of self-confidence

    i. Lack of opportunity to meet men

    j. Demanding perfection in a possible mate

    k. Nursing a disappointment in love

    l. Making an obvious "play" to get a man

3. Be glad you are you.

If we don't like ourselves, no one else will. And furthermore, we may become so preoccupied with worrying about imagined faults that there won't be any energy left to like others.

Better to adopt the attitude proposed by Dr. Harris's popular book *I'm OK—You're OK* (the response of the mature adult, at peace with himself and others).

If you need a model to aid you in developing a positive self-image, it might help to study the lives of outstanding women. Building a composite of the virtues of several successful women should give you an ideal image to identify with. Such a prototype might include the courage of a Helen Keller, the graciousness of a Helen Hayes, the talent of a Grandma Moses, and the sense of direction in life of an Emma Ray McKay.

Do you feel that you are "O.K." now? At peace with yourself? If so, then the next thing to do is to take steps to achieve the goal of getting a husband. How can this be done? Here are some suggestions to consider.

Suggestions for Getting a Husband

(Ideas given by a panel of men and women at a brainstorming session)

1. **How to find your man**

   a. Go where desirable men are. Study areas where there are more men than women. (Large metropolitan centers near graduate schools are good places.)
   b. Attend night school—take courses men like.
   c. Join hiking clubs; take up golf; attend baseball, basketball, and football games.

2. **How to attract him**

   a. Package yourself attractively.
   b. Walk like a happy woman.
   c. Cultivate a pleasing voice.
   d. Smile with your eyes.
   e. Ask him a question.
   f. Radiate happiness and good humor.

3. **How to marry him**

   a. Make him feel important by being sincerely interested in his activities.
   b. Tell him enough about yourself to make him interested, but not so much that you leave nothing in reserve.
   c. Learn to talk about and enjoy the things he likes, such as sports.
   d. Be flexible, and have fun with him on spur-of-the-moment dates that don't cost money.
   e. Engage in church activities with him.
   f. Stick to your moral standards, but convey nonverbal messages to him that you will be a warm and loving wife.
   g. Develop the feeling that you are going in the same direction and have the same lifetime goals.

The above lists are not exhaustive—just long enough

to stimulate your thinking. Undoubtedly you can add many clever ideas of your own.

The point is, if you want to get married, you must do something about it. Try not to sit around and feel sorry for yourself as an "unclaimed jewel." Polish yourself up to your sparkling best and let the whole world know that you want to marry and can bring happiness to some lucky man.

Summary

People who would like to marry should try—

—not to brood over the past.

—to determine what has kept them from marrying.

—to learn to like themselves so others will.

—to get out and meet desirable individuals of the opposite sex.

—to present an attractive self-image.

—to avoid being lusterless, unclaimed jewels, but sparkle so others will enjoy them and be drawn to them by their radiant qualities.

PART FIVE

Choosing a mate

9

Mates Should Inspire
Each Other to Their Best

The late and beloved President David O. McKay once said: "Courtship is a wonderful period. It should be a sacred one. That is the time in which you choose your mate. Your success in life depends upon that choice. Choose prayerfully the one who inspires you to your best."

Author Alexander F. Magoun wrote in his book *Love and Marriage:* "Love is the passionate and abiding desire on the part of two . . . people to produce conditions under which each can be and can spontaneously express his real self: to produce together an intellectual soil and an emotional climate in which each can flourish far superior to what each could achieve alone."

These beautiful thoughts make it quite apparent that marriage should not provide an escape from something, but should offer a relationship in which two people help each other to fulfill life's purposes.

So, if you are planning to marry, try to make sure it is not because you are attempting to—

—escape from an unpleasant situation,
—satisfy sexual desires,
—avoid boredom,
—achieve social status,
—gain economic security.

Marry because you have found the person who inspires you to your best, and be sure you inspire him in the same manner.

Are there any guidelines to help find such a person?

Yes, there are. They are not infallible, because a completely fulfilling marriage requires a lifetime of understanding and adjustment. Nevertheless, studies of successful marital adjustments disclose some things that are important to consider. For example, take your mate-to-be's background. The following factors have been found to be related to happiness in marriage:

1. The degree of happiness of his parents' marriage.

2. His personal happiness in childhood.

3. Harmonious affection with his parents during childhood.

4. Development of a sound attitude toward his sexuality.

Other things that might have a bearing on your future marital hapiness include:

1. A period of acquaintance, courtship, and engagement that is long enough for you to understand each other's attitudes and goals (a minimum engagement period of six months).

2. A mature and similar chronological age. (Marriages with a mate-age difference of over ten years pose additional problems of adjustment.)

3. About the same social and economic background.

4. Ethnic and religious similarities that have produced the same attitudes toward life and standards of conduct.

Should you reject a possible marriage partner if some of these criteria are not fulfilled?

Not necessarily. The above factors are simply guides.

And a man who doesn't meet them all may compensate for their lack by greater motivation to acquire desirable qualities. In other words, if his socioeconomic status is on a different level from yours, you should consider carefully what he has achieved as an individual and the direction in which he is going. It may be that in the future these things will far outweigh the cultural heritage that was more or less handed to him by his parents.

In simple terms, don't rule out the man from the so-called "wrong side of the tracks." Such an arbitrary judgment of an individual's worth is a simplistic evaluation that has no scientific foundation. To put it more succinctly, who has the necessary wisdom to decide which is the "right side of the tracks"?

What about checking a list of desirable personality traits a mate should possess?

Naturally, if you are in the mood to marry, you won't want to be bothered with such lengthy personality checklists and will feel that it is no one else's business what decision you make.

However, it would be wise to consider the following three questions before taking the step.

1. What are my future mate's yesterdays? Is his background compatible with my own?

2. What are my future mate's todays? Do the characteristics that he possesses appeal to me physically, mentally, and spiritually?

3. What are my future mate's tomorrows? Are we both traveling in the same direction? Do we have mutual goals? Do we agree on the purpose of life?

Summary

Choosing a marriage partner is one of our most important decisions in life. We should select one who inspires us to our best. It is wise to learn about our future mate's
—yesterdays
—todays
—tomorrows
And we should seek our Heavenly Father's guidance in prayer.

10

Special Problems
of Remarriage

Those who are planning to remarry after having been widowed or divorced should still seek a mate who inspires them to their best. But they should also be aware that in addition to being compatible marriage partners, they both might have another role to play, that of entering into a family group that has been in operation for some time. Thus, remarriage involves more than choosing the right mate; it also entails adjusting to an established, ongoing social situation.

Disillusionment can occur in a hurry if such factors are not considered. Common laments of those who are unhappy after a second marriage take the form of:

"I thought I married him, not his children."

"I'm treated like an intruder."

"I'm sure he loved his first wife more than he does me."

In a nutshell, the challenge in a second marriage often will be to work out a harmonious relationship between one's self and one's spouse in a family setting that is not always supportive or approving.

Can this really be done?

Yes, it has been done by women and men who have had an awareness of the possible problems and the necessary motivation and capacity to overcome them.

To develop the awareness necessary to make this adjustment, questions to ask are:

Will unhappy experiences or emotional scars from the first marriage affect our attitudes toward each other?

In this relationship, will such mind-sets as carried-over cynicism or hostility toward the other sex hinder good adjustment?

Will either of us tend to idealize (overrate) the good qualities of the first spouse?

If the intended mate does idealize the ex-partner, will you constantly wonder if he or she loves you and feel that you are always being compared unfavorably with the former mate?

Typical of this problem was the attitude dramatically revealed by two of the author's clients in a joint counseling session when the husband turned to his wife and said, "You're not half the woman my first wife was." And the wife replied, "So? My first husband was not a tightwad like you are."

One clue to such a critical attitude on the part of your mate might appear when you start your married life. Will he or she let you select and furnish a new home together or insist that you live in a house that was decorated, furnished, and established by the previous spouse?

Adjustments to Consider

In addition to scrutinizing the attitudes you both will bring to your marriage, there are a number of special adjustments to be made. Important things to consider are:

How will we be received by our new mate's children?

Will friends and relatives accept us both favorably?

Will they cause tension in our marriage because they feel we don't measure up to the former mate?

How do our previous married sex lives compare? Were these behavioral patterns so different that each partner has become accustomed to a type of sexual expression that the other cannot accept?

Why are we marrying each other? For companionship and because we love each other, or for selfish personal reasons?

These are the kinds of questions one must ask one's self to develop the awareness needed to consider with objectivity the commitment to a second marriage.

Possible Financial Problems

It was the second marriage for both partners. The husband, John, was paying alimony and child support to his ex-wife, and the wife, Mary, was receiving alimony and child support from her first husband.

A complicated situation, right?

It was worse than that; it was a hostile stalemate because neither spouse trusted the other. Mary said, "It's none of John's business how much money I receive from my first husband, and I'll spend it the way I please!"

"Mary's completely unreasonable," John commented bitterly. "Why should I tell her how much I'm paying my first wife? After all, I am knocking myself out trying to support two families, and she won't cooperate one tiny bit."

Their hostility toward each other reached a climax in a joint counseling session in my office when Mary asked John for fifty dollars to go shopping.

"I'm sorry, I don't have it," John replied.

"Why, you old skinflint!" sputtered an enraged Mary. Then she jumped up, snatched John's glasses, threw them on the floor, and began pummeling him about the head with her fists. I intervened, and dragged her away from her beleaguered spouse. From that moment on, it was difficult to keep the couple out of the divorce court.

If you are marrying for the second time, you must face the fact that you may have to live within the framework of a complicated financial structure. This is especially true if either of you has been previously divorced. Your husband's alimony and child support payments to his ex-wife may cause you to see red every time the checks are written on the first of the month. You may fume over the problem of living on a reduced income and project the blame for it onto the recipients of the alimony and child support. On the other hand, your husband may resent the way you use the alimony and child support money you receive.

How can you develop an objective attitude toward such monetary problems?

There is only one way. Before your marriage, you and your husband-to-be must be completely honest with each other, lay all of your financial involvements on the table, and see if you can both live with them. If you can view the money that must be expended as a means to an end, that of giving you the opportunity to become companions in the fulfilling of life's purposes, you can do it. On the other hand, if you consider the possession of money to be more important than what is done with it, you will be plagued with financial tensions all of your married life.

The only way to make a go of things is for you both to feel, "We will use our money to achieve our common goals."

Whose Children Are They?

An attractive and childless young wife wept as she said, "I've done everything in my power to be a good mother to my husband's children from his first marriage, but they still reject me. They even refuse to call me mother."

Such situations are quite common, as children from a previous marriage frequently present a challenge in child rearing that some stepparents seem unable to meet. There are mistakes made on both sides. Often children tend to suspect and resist the affections of their new parents, and the parents in turn may resent the children of some other individual and show favoritism to their own.

To overcome this impasse, the new parent should take the intiative. How?

Many of the difficulties and complications can be overcome if both mates will ponder the answer to the question, "Whose children are they?"

Some parents say, "My husband's," "His wife's," or "Mine." Of course, they are really God's. And he has granted all parents the privilege of being his copartners in helping them through the school of life.

Remembering this should give all of us the courage to use our resources in helping each individual child of God achieve the purpose of his existence.

Now we have considered some of the special problems of remarriage, it's up to you to decide if you can successfully meet them. If you are marrying a person who inspires you to your best, you should be able to overcome them together and grow as partners in the kingdom of God.

Summary

Those who remarry should—
—seek a mate who inspires them to do their
   best.
—be aware that they will play the dual role
   of adjusting to their new mate and an
   established family.
—discuss their financial obligations honest-
   ly with each other, and make money their
   servant, rather than their master.
—realize that all children are God's, and it is
   their privilege to help each one achieve
   life's purposes.
—look upon their new marriage as an opportunity to continue growing in God's
   kingdom.

11

Temple Marriage—Each Individual's Decision

A spirit of peace and quiet serenity filled the room as the happy couple faced each other at the temple altar. As they were pronounced husband and wife forever and ever, an expression of love mingled with joy appeared on their faces.

After the ceremony, fathers and mothers, brothers and sisters, and other loving relatives embraced them and wished them eternal happiness. One could almost sense God's approval of the event, and it was indeed a scene to remember.

If you are planning to marry or remarry, you should not deny yourself the blessings of a temple marriage.

However, it must be remembered that being united for time and eternity in a temple of God is a privilege reserved only for those couples who qualify. In other words, you both must be active, faithful members of the Church and have your bishop and stake president affirm this with temple recommends after interviewing you. **The requirements you must meet to be married in the temple are:**

Both partners must be baptized and confirmed members of the Church.

The man must hold the Melchizedek Priesthood.

Each must be interviewed individually by his bishop and stake president and asked the following questions:

1. Are you morally clean and worthy to enter the temple?

2. Will you and do you sustain the General Authorities of the Church, and will you live in accordance with the accepted rules and doctrines of the Church?

3. Do you have any connection, in sympathy or otherwise, with any of the apostate groups or individuals who are running counter to the accepted rules and doctrines of the Church?

4. Are you a full tithe payer?

5. Do you keep the Word of Wisdom?

6. Will you wear the regulation garments?

7. Will you earnestly strive to do your duty in the Church, to attend your sacrament, priesthood, and other meetings, and to obey the rules, laws, and commandments of the gospel?

8. Have you ever been denied a recommend to any temple?

9. Have you ever been divorced?

At the conclusion of these interviews, if it is the judgment of the bishop and the stake president that you are worthy to enter the temple, each of you will be given a recommend to the temple presidency for admission.

Two other things must be kept in mind. Each of you must receive your temple endowments (your bishop will explain these to you) before the marriage ceremony. This may be done on or before the day of the marriage.

Your marriage date and time must be arranged ahead, to learn when your ceremony can take place and who will be available to perform it.

You must remember also that before being married in the temple, you must comply with the requirements of the civil marriage laws of the state or country in which the temple is located. Such requirements may include a blood test.

If either of you has been previously divorced, you must go through this additional procedure before receiving a temple recommend: The bishop obtains the facts about the divorce and submits them to the First Presidency. They review the divorce circumstances, and if they feel the facts justify it, a letter is sent to the bishop authorizing the issuance of a temple recommend if you are considered worthy after a careful interview by the bishop and stake president. If a woman has been married in the temple previously, the First Presidency must also cancel her previous sealing before she proceeds. A man married in the temple who has had a civil divorce but not a cancellation of the sealing may be recommended for temple marriage without having the previous sealing annulled if he is fully worthy and if his divorce has been cleared by the First Presidency.

In addition to following the general procedures to receive a temple recommend, if you are a widow and were married in the temple to your deceased husband, you may not enter a temple marriage with a second man, as you are sealed for eternity to your first husband.

A widower who receives a temple recommend may, with the approval of the Church authorities, enter into a second temple marriage.

Is a Temple Marriage Worth the Effort?

You may wonder if a temple marriage is not too much fuss and bother and say, as some others do, "I'm concerned with being happy right now. Eternity is too far away to worry about."

All that can be said in rebuttal is, that is indeed your choice to make, but try to withhold your decision until you consider the following advantages of a temple marriage.

1. Your temple marriage increases your chances for happiness right now, because both of you need to know each other well enough to make a permanent commitment.

2. You are entering a partnership with God, and he will bless you if you honor your contract.

3. It provides the way for being with your husband and children throughout eternity.

4. The beautiful and sacred experience will become a memory to buoy you up in times of trial.

5. You and your family will share in the blessings of the priesthood to guide and sustain you in your home.

6. Your temple marriage makes it possible for you and your husband to aspire to godhood.

Do you really want to pass up these advantages of a temple marriage? If so, for what? A marriage that will be dissolved with death? No assurance that your children will be yours in the hereafter? Undefined possibilities for eternal progression? Depriving yourselves of sharing the blessings of a special partnership with God?

Now, which path do you choose to follow? Search the depths of your soul and pray to your Father in heaven before you decide.

Summary

Qualifying for a temple marriage is a privilege reserved for the dedicated and the faithful.

A temple marriage gives each couple a blueprint for now and eternity.

It eliminates the insecurity of a temporary marriage commitment.

It provides the way for an eternal family relationship.

It is a step pleasing to God. He will bless those who take it.

PART SIX

Guidelines to
confident living

12

Our Eternal Destiny

Paul Harvey, the dynamic news commentator, recently said, "There is a human craving for something transcendent. Religious tradition for thousands of years knew the meaning of life and the purpose of death and the individual's proper place in the here and hereafter.

"Now a vacillating, contradicting, codeless 'modern' church has compounded our confusion and left in the place it once filled, a vast, dark emptiness."

Mr. Harvey's statement accurately portrays the state of many of today's churches. There is confusion among them, and a vacillating approach in defining the purpose of life. However, this popular personality overlooks the fact that the Church of Jesus Christ has always taught the same truths that the Savior taught during his ministry. We who are members of The Church of Jesus Christ of Latter-day Saints know that there is not "a vast, dark emptiness," that God's church is still upon the earth, and that through his revelations to his servants he is constantly explaining the meaning of life and the purpose of death to us.

But just how strong is our testimony of these things?

Does it weaken when the sailing on life's waters becomes rough?

Do we find ourselves saying, "Why did this happen to me?" and begin to doubt the goodness of God when personal misfortune strikes?

Perhaps you remember the motion picture *The Unsinkable Molly Brown*, in which actress Debbie Reynolds portrayed an individual who met adversity with unflinching courage. This is the kind of courage we all need, that which makes us unsinkable. Such courage comes from an unshakable testimony which can be built and maintained by doing three things:

1. *Believing that God knows all things and can control all things.*

Such faith was demonstrated by a woman in South America. As an earthquake shook everything around, and others cringed with terror, she calmly said, "Isn't it wonderful that God has the power to even make the earth tremble."

And by the faithful sister facing critical surgery who remarked, "I hope God will let me live long enough to raise my small boys to adulthood."

2. *Keeping in touch with God through prayer.*

At one time I was visiting a sister who had been beset with one misfortune after another, and during the course of the conversation I made the comment, "It's amazing to me how you can keep going."

"It shouldn't be," she said, blue eyes flashing. "I talk things over with God, and he always helps me."

Such individuals who make prayer a part of their lives suggest the following things that work for them: (a) express gratitude, (b) ask for guidance, and (c) work with a will to do God's will.

3. *Developing a long-range view—an eternal perspective of life.*

The LDS concept of eternal life, as revealed by God, is that after the resurrection each individual will dwell in a world that is commensurate with how he has kept God's commandments on this earth.

The most highly prized dwelling place, the celestial world, will be inhabited by those "who have received of his fulness, and of his glory." They have kept the commandments and "shall dwell in the presence of God and his Christ forever and ever."

The other two lesser worlds, the terrestrial and the telestial, will be the dwelling places of those who have not been as "valiant in the testimony of Jesus" (terrestrial) and "they who received not the gospel of Christ, neither the testimony of Jesus" (telestial). (See Doctrine and Covenants 76.)

Some single women say that what bothers them is that to reach the highest glory in the celestial world, or kingdom, a woman must enter the new and everlasting covenant (Doctrine and Covenants 132) and be married and sealed to a man for time and eternity in a temple of God.

Those who are single or have married a man who cannot qualify for temple marriage make comments such as, "It seems unfair that I will be denied these blessings. I have been active and faithful in the Church all of my life, so why should I be held back in the hereafter because I have not been married in the temple?"

It is natural to feel this way, but it will help those who are single to remember that God loves them and has promised all of us the blessings that come from keeping his commandments. He has even said, "I am bound if you do what I say"—that is, keep his commandments.

Thus, the task that faces us is to live righteously and trust in God's promises.

Church leaders have made it clear that no one will be denied any present or future blessings if he or she lives according to God's commandments. President Brigham Young wrote, "Many of the sisters grieve because they are not blessed with offspring. You will see the time when you will have millions of children around you. If you are

faithful to your covenants, you will be mothers of na-
tions." (*Discourses of Brigham Young,* p. 310.)

Elder Melvin J. Ballard said, "Now then, what of your
daughters who have died and have not been sealed to
some man? . . . The sealing power shall be forever and
ever with this church, and provisions will be made for
them. . . . Their blessings and privileges will come to them
in due time." ("Three Degrees of Glory," discourse de-
livered in the Ogden Tabernacle, September 2, 1922.)

President Harold B. Lee offers the following reassuring words:

"The Lord judges us not alone by the things we do
but by the intent of our hearts . . . the Lord said, all those
who have died without a knowledge of this Gospel, who
would have received it had they been permitted to tarry,
shall be heirs of the celestial kingdom of God. (See *Doc-
umentary History of the Church,* vol. 2, p. 280.)

"Thus, wives and mothers who have been denied the
blessings of wifehood or motherhood in this life—who say
in their hearts, if I could have done, I would have done,
or I would give if I had, but I cannot for I have not—the
Lord will bless you as though you had done, and the
world to come will compensate for those who desire in
their hearts the righteous things that they were not able
to do because of no fault of their own." (*Ensign,* February
1972, p. 56.)

President Joseph Fielding Smith promised future
blessings to faithful single women. He wrote:

"You good sisters, who are single and alone, do not
fear, do not feel that blessings are going to be withheld
from you. You are not under any obligation or necessity
of accepting some proposal that comes to you which is distasteful for fear you will come under condemnation. If in
your hearts you feel that the gospel is true, and would
under proper conditions receive these ordinances and
sealing blessings in the temple of the Lord: and that is
your faith and your hope and your desire, and that does

not come to you now; the Lord will make it up, and you shall be blessed—for no blessing shall be withheld.

"The Lord will judge you according to the desires of your hearts when blessings are withheld in this life, and he is not going to condemn you for that which you cannot help." (*Doctrines of Salvation*, Bookcraft, 1955, vol. 2, p. 76.)

These beautiful and reassuring thoughts make it apparent that we all will be taken care of in God's scheme of things, if we do our part and keep his commandments. It will help along the way if we remember that our Heavenly Father is a God of order and will see that everything is taken care of in its proper time. Consequently, the time to marry is not necessarily the same for everyone.

This thought is expressed beautifully in the Bible:

"To every thing there is a season, and a time to every purpose under the heaven:

"A time to love, and a time to hate; a time of war, and a time of peace.

"I know that there is no good . . . but for a man to rejoice, and to do good in his life." (Ecclesiastes 3:1, 8, 12.)

Keeping these thoughts constantly in our minds will give us an inner peace that will enable us to cope with the tensions and pressures of contemporary society and surmount the obstacles that we meet on our way to the celestial kingdom.

Our eternal destiny? To "dwell in the presence of God and his Christ forever and ever" and to become gods and goddesses, if we will.

Summary

An unshakable testimony that God knows all things and can control all things will help make us unsinkable on the sea of life.

Prayer will help us to work with a will and do God's will.

If we, as individuals, stay on the road to the celestial kingdom and keep the commandments, all blessings will be ours.

"To every thing there is a season." The time to marry is not the same for everyone.

Inner peace comes from keeping busy within the long-range eternal framework of the gospel.

We can become gods and goddesses, if we will.

13

How to Find Friends
with Mutual Interests

One of the most difficult things facing a widowed, divorced, or older single woman or man is to find a circle of congenial friends who have mutual interests. If you have such a problem, there are a number of organizations that are ready, willing, and able to help you. As a Latter-day Saint, you naturally wonder if the Church has such an organization. It does, and it's a good one.

The Special Interests program of the Church, approved by the First Presidency and the General Authorities, was organized in 1969 to serve the widowed, divorced, and older single members of the Church. The program, designed now as a function of the Melchizedek Priesthood Mutual Interests Association, is structured to supplement the cultural, spiritual, social, and educational needs of single adults.

It is put into operation as follows:

The stake president appoints a stake committee consisting of a high councilor, with his wife assisting, and a Special Interests representative. Each ward bishop is also instructed to appoint a representative to promote activity within the ward.

Each stake makes a survey to identify and involve Special Interests members. Such surveys show large numbers of potential members. One stake has 904, and some wards have as many as 200 widows on their membership lists. In addition, personality profiles and the individual interests of each potential member are obtained and tabulated. After this information is all in, group activities for members are put into motion. These activities might include:

· Stake firesides to get acquainted and hear selected speakers and discussions.

· Weekly or monthly stake, regional, or multiregional dances.

· Parties, such as bowling, snowmobiling, potluck dinners, progressive dinners, Christmas get-togethers, roller skating, picnics, group sports activities and group attendance to view baseball, football, basketball, hockey, golf, tennis, and other sports.

· Group attendance at symphonies, concerts, plays, lectures, museums, art exhibits, book reviews, and other events of a cultural nature.

· Small weekly group discussions related to rearing children in a one-parent home (for those involved in the single-parent situation).

· Family home evenings composed of six to eight one-parent families (with permission of the bishop).

· Home evenings for small groups of single adults.

· A fellowshiping program for elderly widows or widowers living away from children and grandchildren, in which a Special Interests member visits or phones frequently to ask, "How are you? May we help you today?"

· A designated member to send cards and arrange parties on members' birthdays.

· A telephone answering service, which a member may dial anytime he or she feels the need to talk to someone.

· Group bus tours to scenic spots, popular resorts, and places of historical and religious interest. (If you think such trips are impractical, you may be surprised to learn that one Special Interests group recently made a Caribbean cruise.)

After scanning the endless possibilities the Church Special Interests program offers for meeting congenial people with interests similar to yours, how is the best way to become involved? Telephone your bishop and he will tell you.

Other Programs

In the event you live in an area where Church membership is too small to provide such a program, do not become discouraged, as there are organizations outside the Church that are designed to bring together people who have mutual interests. The functions of two typical ones are given below, followed by a list of the names of several others.

The first of these groups is Parents Without Partners, Inc., an organization with headquarters at 80 Fifth Avenue, New York, N.Y. 10011. The following information is reprinted by permission of the executive officers of Parents Without Partners. (Copyright 1967.)

WHO ARE WE?

We are an international organization of single parents—widowed, divorced, separated or never married—who, since the first Chapter was organized in 1957, have come together for mutual help so that our single-parent homes can better provide a happy family environment in which to bring up our children.

Our purposes are basically educational: with professional help, we conduct a program in which lectures, discussions, publications and recreational activities aid the individual single parent to cope with the many problems and dilemmas that must be faced in a single-parent home.

In 1958, we were chartered by the State of New York as a non-profit membership corporation. Since that time we have grown rapidly, and now have Chapters in every corner of the United States, in Canada, and in other countries.

WHAT DO WE DO?

Both the international organization, and the many individual Chapters, carry on programs and activities to help single parents and their children.

PWP International, with headquarters in New York City, charters the individual Chapters, supervises the educational programs conducted by Chapters, and—

· Publishes *The Single Parent* magazine, which is the only publication dealing solely with the problems of single-parenthood. Featured are articles on such topics as child-rearing, income taxes, remarriage, psychological problems and adjustments, education, and a host of others.

· Prepares and distributes educational material and program aids to the Chapters, and a monthly bulletin.

· Authorizes and conducts research into the many unexplored areas of single-parent living.

· Conducts annual International Conferences, and supervises the many Zone and Regional Conferences that take place during the year.

· Maintains close relationships with, and seeks the help of, professional people concerned with our special areas of interest, and works with educational institutions to improve our programs and activities.

· Through a dynamic informational program, brings single-parent problems to the attention of the public and of government agencies.

Individual Chapters organize and conduct educational programs to fit the needs of their members. They do this through—

· Monthly educational programs, with professional speakers and panelists, on such subjects as "How to Live as a Single Parent"; "Parent-Child Relationships in a One-Parent Home"; "Sex Education for Children," etc.

· Discussion groups, usually professionally-led, at which members "talk out" their problems and share experiences with each other. Some Discussion Groups may be planned only for the widowed, or the divorced or separated, but others can deal with specific topics such as, "Remarriage"; "Dating and Relating"; "How to Deal with Loneliness," etc.

· Chapter Newsletters, containing a calendar of events plus information useful to the single parent.

· Recreational and social activities for both adults and children, providing a comfortable environment for recreation free of the "fifth wheel" feeling.

WHAT PWP CAN DO FOR YOU

Our society is based on the traditional 2-parent home, and is not equipped for, nor does it really understand, the special problems faced by the millions who must bring up their children alone. Parents Without Partners, Inc. is uniquely fitted to help you, because our members themselves have gone through and experienced the despair and discouragement that accompany the loss of a mate, and the struggle to re-establish a new kind of life.

PWP *can* help you. You will find sympathetic and understanding people with whom you can share your experiences, problems and hopes. You can gain a new perspective on yourself as you discover that you are not alone, and that others have triumphed over the same kind of difficulties you are facing. You can learn to accept what you *must*, while you strive toward a more successful way of life.

Your children need not be "victims" of the one-parent situation. From the new insights you can gain, you can be a better parent, and your children will benefit—not only from the activities planned for them, but from the new strength and self-reliance you can derive from the educational program and your association with friendly people "in the same boat."

HOW CAN YOU JOIN?

IF THERE IS a PWP Chapter in your community, or nearby, your active membership will be welcomed. Simply call or write the local Chapter. (To be eligible for membership, you must be a parent, and widowed, divorced, separated or never married.)

If you do not know where Chapters are located, drop a note to our New York headquarters. Addresses of Chapters near you will be sent promptly.

If no Chapter exists in your area, you can lend your support to PWP, Inc. by becoming an *Associate Member*. You will receive *The Single Parent* magazine, and will be eligible to attend functions at any PWP Chapter. Write our New York headquarters for application forms.

WHY NOT FORM
A PWP CHAPTER?

NEW CHAPTERS ARE constantly being chartered. If no Chapter exists in your community, we invite you to take steps to form one.

With a minimum of 15 new members, you may obtain a charter from Parents Without Partners, Inc. You will find that founding a PWP Chapter is a rewarding experience, and you will derive the great satisfaction of knowing that you have brought help to the many single parents in your community who so urgently need help.

A note to our New York headquarters will

bring information promptly. You will be aided in your organizing efforts by the Zone Director, the Regional Director and the State Director, who supervise PWP activities in your area, as well as by the enthusiastic members of nearby Chapters of Parents Without Partners, Inc.

POINTS FOR SINGLE PARENTS

1. Allow yourself and your children time for readjustment —a convalescence from an emotional operation, whether from death or divorce, is essential.

2. Remember, it is not a sign of weakness but of strength to know one needs help and to be able to accept it. Seek it from old friends, from PWP, from professionals.

3. Examine your motives to see if they stem from self-pity, jealousy, blaming or getting-even. If they do, you will have to change them in order to be more successful in building a good home and a new life.

4. Remember the best parts of your marriage but without living in the past. Share them with your children and use them constructively to build toward another marriage.

5. Share some of your feelings with your children and let them share theirs with you. Be on guard, however, against imposing yours on them or demanding their confidences. Remember that the feelings and perceptions of children for parents can never be the same as spouse for spouse.

6. Remember that your attitudes toward yourself and missing partner may make the difference between your child's good or poor adjustment to the new one-parent situation. Beware of impeding your children's growth by over-protecting or over-burdening them.

7. If you want the respect and love of your children, you must allow them to respect and love the other parent. This means not belittling or continuing the battle, as well as encouraging visits. Beware condemning your children because they remind you of the other parent.

8. Reassure your children that they are not being rejected —that the other parent still loves them. Your complaints may be interpreted by them as rejection.

9. Make an effort to think of yourself as an individual and not as a part of someone else. Dependency, which you

thought outgrown, may be lurking in hidden recesses. The value you place on yourself will be reflected in your children and friends.

10. Use your single status as an oportunity for growth and development—make each day count by trying something new or making new friends. Remember that your new situation will change old relationships and lead to new ones.

OUR GOALS ★

As conscientious single parents, it is our primary endeavor to bring our children to healthy maturity, with the full sense of being loved and accepted as persons, and with the same prospects for normal adulthood as children who mature with their two parents together.

From the divorce or separation which divides a family, or the loss of a parent by death, it is the child who suffers most. For children in such circumstances to grow unscarred requires the utmost in love, understanding and sound guidance. To provide these is a responsibility inherent in parenthood. It does not end with separation or divorce, for either parent.

The single parent in our society is isolated to some degree. The difficulties of providing both for ourselves and our children a reasonable equivalent of normal life, is increased by that isolation. The established pattern of community life lacks both means of communication and institutions to enable us to resolve our special problems, and find normal fulfillment.

Therefore, in the conviction that we can achieve this and, through working together, through the exchange of ideas, and through the mutual understanding, help and companionship which we find with one another, we have established "PARENTS WITHOUT PARTNERS, INC," to further our common welfare and the well-being of our children. . . .

*From the Constitution of Parents Without Partners, Inc., a nonprofit membership corporation chartered on March 12, 1958.

Another organization is Neurotics Anonymous, a group of people banded together to solve their emotional problems. Their headquarters are: Room 426, Colorado Building, 1341 G Street N.W., Washington, D.C. 20005.

This organization does not use the word *neurotic* in its scientific sense; it defines a neurotic as "any person whose emotions interfere with his functioning in any way and to any degree whatsoever as recognized by him." Some of their suggestions are as follows (reprinted by permission of the executive officers of Neurotics Anonymous):

JUST FOR TODAY

JUST FOR TODAY I will try to live through this day only, and not tackle my whole life problem at once. I can do something for twelve hours that would appall me if I felt that I had to keep it up for a lifetime.

JUST FOR TODAY I will be happy. This assumes to be true what Abraham Lincoln said, that, "Most folks are as happy as they make up their minds to be."

JUST FOR TODAY I will adjust myself to what is, and not try to adjust everything to my own desires. I will take my luck as it comes and fit myself to it.

JUST FOR TODAY I will try to strengthen my mind. I will study. I will learn something useful. I will not be a mental loafer. I will read something that requires effort, thought and concentration.

JUST FOR TODAY I will exercise my soul in three ways: I will do somebody a good turn, and not get found out; if anybody knows of it, it will not count. I will do at least two things I don't want to do—just for exercise. I will not show anyone that my feelings are hurt; they may be hurt, but today I will not show it.

JUST FOR TODAY I will be agreeable. I will look as well as I can, dress becomingly, talk low, act courteously, criticize not one bit, not find fault with anything, and not try to improve or regulate anybody except myself.

JUST FOR TODAY I will have a program. I may not follow it exactly, but I will have it. I will save myself from two pests: hurry and indecision.

JUST FOR TODAY I will have a quiet half hour all by myself, and relax. During this half hour, sometime, I will try and get a better perspective of my life.

JUST FOR TODAY I will be unafraid. Especially I will not be afraid to enjoy what is beautiful, and to believe that as I give to the world, so the world will give to me.

THE TWELVE SUGGESTED STEPS OF NEUROTICS ANONYMOUS

1—We admitted we were powerless over our emotions—that our lives had become unmanageable.

2—Came to believe that a Power greater than ourselves could restore us to sanity.

3—Made a decision to turn our will and our lives over to the care of God *as we understood Him.*

4—Made a searching and fearless moral inventory of ourselves.

5—Admitted to God, to ourselves and to another human being the exact nature of our wrongs.

6—Were entirely ready to have God remove all these defects of character.

7—Humbly asked Him to remove our shortcomings.

8—Made a list of all persons we had harmed, and became willing to make amends to them all.

9—Made direct amends to such people wherever possible, except when to do so would injure them or others.

10—Continued to take personal inventory and when we were wrong promptly admitted it.

11—Sought through prayer and meditation to improve our conscious contact with God *as we understood Him,* praying only for knowledge of His will for us and the power to carry that out.

12—Having had a spiritual awakening as the result of these steps, we tried to carry this message to neurotics, and to practice these principles in all our affairs.

SLOGANS WE USE:

1. Let go and let God
2. You are not alone
3. Easy does it
4. Live and let live
5. First things first
6. Look for the good

7. THINK—THINK—THINK
8. But for the Grace of God
9. Three A's
   a. Acceptance
   b. Awareness
   c. Action

Other Helpful Organizations

LDS Church Social Services: For counseling and help of all types.

LDS Employment Service, State Employment Services, Departments of Vocational Rehabilitation: Offer assistance in job training and procurement.

City and County Mental Health Clinics: Give assistance in solving emotional problems on an individual or group basis.

Community Chest, United Fund, Chamber of Commerce, Civic Council: Provide referral services to reputable agencies and individual practitioners.

County Welfare Departments: Offer emotional help and material assistance.

Legal Aid Society: Gives help with legal problems.

National Council on Family Relations: Provides literature and classes for single persons. Family-oriented organization with state affiliates.

Solo Parents: Functions in the same manner as Parents Without Partners.

Tip-Toppers: Organized for the tall single girl.

Universities and Schools: Sponsor special classes and activities.

Young Women's Christian Association (YWCA): Provides special classes and sponsors group activities for single men and women.

Summary

We can find congenial friends with mutual interests if we make the effort.

The LDS Special Interests program offers unlimited possibilities for acquiring friends and becoming involved in interesting activities.

For those who live in an area where Church membership is too small for this program, there are other organizations ready to help.

Individuals need not feel alone or isolated. We should all seek others with mutual interests and travel life's two-way street of giving joy to others and receiving in kind.

14

Cherishing Womanhood

Each sex, male and female, has a unique role to play in life. Research studies of sex differences show that women and men have been created to complement and not compete with each other. Here are a few of the differences.

Anatomical Differences

Men
• Are usually larger and stronger, with more immediate strength.

• Have 10 percent more red corpuscles, redder blood, more hemoglobin, which transports oxygen around the body and delivers it where it is needed. Are less sensitive to pain, pressure, heat, etc.

Women
• Are more durable, have greater endurance over long periods of time.

• Can renew their blood more easily, have better chance for recovery from accidents.

• Bear pain and pressure and endure cold better.

· Have fewer glandular problems.

· Have heavier blood and slower heartbeat, and thus a greater need for oxygen.

· Have smaller lungs and hearts, need less oxygen, resist poisonous fumes better.

Mental and Emotional Differences

Men

· Think more concretely; for example, in preparing a tax report or a blueprint of a house.

· Native intelligence same as in women.

· More frequently have psychopathic personalities, evidencing impulsive and antisocial behavior and lack of control.

Women

· Better in abstract thinking; for example, in providing a list of wedding anniversaries or historical data.

· Girls mature more rapidly intellectually.

· More frequently suffer from neurosis. Tend to be more anxious, fearful, and subject to depression.

Much more could be written about the differences between men and women, but the few examples given here should indicate that neither sex is superior. Each has strengths the other lacks, all of which bear out the fact that woman's role in this world is to be an equal-status companion to man, not a competitor.

Still, a woman has a unique role that a man cannot fill. Just as every cell in her body is different from a man's, so is her place in life. Unfortunately, some contemporary women don't realize this and are mistakenly attempting to play male roles.

Just what is a woman's role?

William Shakespeare wrote, "Women are the books,

the arts, the academics, that show, contain, and nourish all the world."

Martin Luther said that her role is to be "mother of all living creatures."

May we add that woman's unchanging and everlasting role is to nourish God's children spiritually and guide them lovingly as they strive to reach heaven.

We are sure that you as a woman cherish this role. No one else can fill it.

Loving Ourselves

A middle-aged woman whose husband had left her to bring up her eight children by herself sparkled with enthusiasm as she reported her activities as a playground director. When she had finished, the students in the writer's Personal Adjustment class began to question her:

"Why are you so happy? You said you don't make much money."

"Aren't you tired out managing a home with eight children and holding a full-time job?"

"You say you have little time for social life and you think the chances for remarriage are nil? Just what is it that helps you face life with such enthusiasm?"

This fascinating lady stood tall, stretching her five-foot-two frame to its limits, and smiled as she replied, "I like being a woman and I like myself. I like people, especially children, and I like what I'm doing. To me that spells happiness."

The students had no rebuttals. As the bell rang and they filed from the classroom, one could hear them uttering phrases of admiration for the woman, who was over twice their age and not half as attractive physically (by Hollywood standards). She had won them over with her inner beauty.

Inner beauty is the kind of beauty that lasts a lifetime, and it doesn't come from using false eyelashes or other external beauty aids. Rather, it is the beauty that God gives to us as his children.

Understanding this is what helped Vonda Kay Van Dyke become Miss America in 1965. When she was interviewed, she said, "The real beauty in every girl is an elusive inner quality that has to be carefully and prayerfully developed. Only its potential is yours at birth, and you can't ever see it or touch it. It's more of an image—God's image of you. . . . God will always see your real beauty . . . and even though the world is nearsighted, it needs the beauty God sees in you. It needs to see that inner promise fulfilled in your everyday life. If you can begin to live up to God's best hopes for you, the world will know what you are—a truly beautiful person." (Vonda Kay Van Dyke, *That Girl in Your Mirror*, Fleming H. Revell Co., 1966, p. 41.)

Our inner beauty won't help others much unless we use it in a pleasant manner. Others will be more likely to tune in to it if we think happy thoughts. How many times have you heard a beautiful—yes, inwardly beautiful —woman or a good man speak in church without using one single smile? The message was there, but being presented with cold logic, it didn't radiate warmth to the audience. Was it because the speaker felt it was undignified or not spiritual to smile? What a shame! We shouldn't make the same mistake. Think happy today.

In addition to helping our communication with others, thinking happy thoughts will also enhance our appearance. In fact, it will do more for facial beauty than a dozen jars of cold cream.

You doubt this? Here's an illustration of how it works. Having had the opportunity of traveling extensively in Europe, the writer has seen numerous peasant men and women working in the fields. These hard-working people seem to have unusual strength and physical endurance, yet with few exceptions their faces seem sad and old. Why? Because of extreme hardship, they have tended to lose sight of their unique roles as individuals, have lost their inner glow, and have sadly resigned themselves to what they feel is a dreary life.

Don't misunderstand, we are not judging these people, but simply pointing out that circumstances that have crowded happy thoughts out of their minds have also aged their facial appearance.

Someone has written that "nobody is responsible for his face up to the age of thirty. From then on he shapes it." Scientific research corroborates this by suggesting that aging of the features depends upon the facial expression.

We should remember that facial expression is the barometer of the emotional climate in which we live, and sadness and happiness put different kinds of marks on the countenance.

Naturally, it is difficult to think happily all of the time, but progress can be made in that direction by using three golden keys:

1. *Substitute happy, constructive thoughts for unhappy thoughts.* Rain is miserable and ugly—or rain makes things green and beautiful. Nighttime frightens me—or nighttime gives me comforting rest. Being alone depresses me —or being alone is a relief from bustle. My refrigerator is half empty—or my refrigerator is half full. God is punishing me—or God is giving me an opportunity to grow.

2. *Substitute creative thoughts for plodding thoughts.* Our imagination can help keep us happy if we stir it up and use it properly. Entering the world of fantasy can be exhilarating and rejuvenating, providing we can leave it at will.

One of the most delightful and rejuvenating days of my life was spent recently at Disney World in Florida. My wife, Elise, and I had the good fortune of seeing this world of fantasy with some dear friends, Harmon and Elaine Killebrew and their family.

What a delight! Walt Disney's Magic Kingdom kept us and fifty thousand others enthralled hour after hour. And it was all based on fantasy. It is said that as Walt Disney lay dying, he called in his brother and told him he could visualize on the ceiling of his hospital room just how Disney World should be laid out.

Mankind has been provided with immeasurable happiness as the result of one man's imagination.

In order to exercise creative thinking we should try
to—

   a. Take a few minutes each day to dream of things
we would like to do; put them down on a pad and
later weigh their possible value.

   b. Associate with children and try to see the world
through their eyes.

   c. Be alert to new sights and sounds. Can we use
them? A famous writer wrote a story about a piece
of string that he saw lying on the ground.

   d. Study the people we see; try to determine their
profession, personality, etc., from their appearance.

   e. Use our own observations and experiences to illustrate principles in speeches we give.

   f. Give ourselves a deadline for the use of specific
constructive ideas we dream about.

   3. *Give our happy thoughts to others.* Someone has said,
"That which we give away we keep." Expressing a happy
thought to someone else will fix it more firmly in one's
mind. Acting on a happy thought will help us as well as
others.

To summarize, we should cherish our manhood and
our womanhood; and think, give away, and act on happy
thoughts. If we do, our inner beauty will help illuminate
the pathways to happiness that everyone is seeking.

Summary

No one else can fill one's unique role as an individual.

Thinking happy thoughts will give us a start on the road to happiness.

We must love ourselves before we can love others.

If we cherish our personhood, our inner beauty will light the way for others.

15

Managing Our Emotions

"The spirit within me is greater than this earth and sky and the heaven and all these united." (Ancient Hindu saying.)

Our spirit is indeed the driving force within us, but to have it steer a straight course to heaven, we must learn to manage our emotions. This is no easy task, because we are born to conflict.

Theological doctrine tells us that life is a constant battle between resisting the influence of the adversary and following the teachings of our Lord and Savior, Jesus Christ.

We are counseled to pray constantly, search the scriptures, and keep active in the Church in order to maintain the strength to resist evil. Such practice is considered necessary if we would master our emotions.

Psychoanalytic theory teaches the same thing, using slightly different terminology. It is postulated that a baby is in conflict with its environment from the moment it is born: its inner drives (contained in the unbridled id) are seeking expression, and environmental pressures (parental guidance and teachings) are denying them an outlet. Thus it takes the child a few years to adjust to this conflict by acquiring sound standards (a conscience) to live by and learning to channel instinctive drives into acceptable behavioral patterns. A somewhat different type of conflict exists within the individual during adulthood, that of keeping emotions in balance.

Most individuals have a conscience, but they have difficulty following it when their emotions interfere.

Why do we become angry and say something we immediately regret? Or sulk and refuse to continue talking to our best friend? Why do we do it? Surely we know better.

The reason is that our emotions suddenly block our thinking, and our years of training in how to get along with people fall by the wayside.

Emotional outbursts not only disrupt ongoing behavior, but chronic emotional states, brought about by conditions such as anxiety, often make it difficult to complete long-range tasks. Emotions such as fear, anger, and anxiety also have the properties of drives. Fear may lead to escape behavior, anger to aggressive responses, and anxiety to many kinds of harmful activities.

It naturally follows that it is necessary to control our emotions, even a positive one like love, if we would strive toward perfection and possible godhood. But how?

Psychological Control of Emotions

To start, let's look at the control of emotions from a psychological and a spiritual standpoint.

The word *emotion* is derived from the Latin word *emovere*, which means "to move," "to stir," or "to mix." Thus, we could say that an emotion is a stirred-up state of the individual in a particular way with accompanying changes in subjective feelings, perception, and motivation, and usually (although not always) observable behavior.

Psychologically speaking, this stirred-up condition occurs when a person experiences a sensation, from a visual or other type of experience. Then the nervous system functions as follows: The cerebrum (the remembering and reasoning part of the brain, based on the individual's previous learning experience) determines what emotion, if any, is called for. Subsequently, impulses are sent to other parts of the brain, principally the hypothalamus, the seat of emotional expressions. Then the autonomic nervous system sets off certain changes in the body.

Psychologists have different theories about the function of this "stirring up." One, the "emergency theory," which is widely accepted, postulates that man needs to mobilize all his physical resources to met certain emergency occasions and to be ready to fight, run away, or make an objective adjustment to the situation.

Although these psychological theories are confusing, they do give us some clues related to how our spiritual selves can control our emotions.

First, we should realize that emotions are natural parts of our make-up that can also be desirable if controlled. The scriptures tell us that even God experiences emotions, such as anger.

"I, the Lord, was angry with you yesterday, but today mine anger is turned away." (Doctrine and Covenants 61: 20.)

"Be ye angry, and sin not: let not the sun go down upon your wrath: Neither give place to the devil." (Ephesians 4:26-27.)

It is clear from these verses that the emotion of anger itself is not a sin, but the harm comes from staying angry and using anger to hurt others.

Thus it follows that controlled emotions can be used for good purposes. Undoubtedly, great books have been written because of anger over injustice, and the world has been made better by those who have controlled and guided emotions of anger, love, fear, and others into constructive channels.

The Need for Spiritual Self-Control

So, how can our spiritual self control these powerful feelings that are called emotions?

We might use the following analogy.

As children of God, all of our spirits are in contact with a central switchboard (the light of the gospel) that allows us to communicate with him. In turn, within our bodies we have a subsidiary network of circuits that enables us to transmit external influences to our spirit, which, in turn, sends out messages telling us how we should behave in relationship to these influences.

If our spirit keeps plugged into the central switchboard (enjoys God's Spirit) and the network of communications within ourselves is functioning effectively, we can control our emotions. But if our wires of communication become crossed or contact with the general switchboard becomes jammed, we lose control of our emotions and trouble develops.

It is obvious, then, that the basic way to control emotions is to keep in tune with God. However, learning specific ways of meeting emotional situations is also important, so we can keep our communication system to God from getting out of order.

Parents and teachers play an important role in this learning. If they teach effectively, we learn that there are fundamental principles of living that we cannot violate if we desire a happy and abundant life. Such principles include self-control, loving ourselves and others, and trying to see the other person's viewpoint so we won't judge him unfairly.

Keeping in tune with God's Spirit through the central switchboard and practicing the Christlike principles of understanding and doing good to others should enable us to keep our emotions under control.

Now let's apply the foregoing discussion to our future behavior. When our emotions seem to be getting out of hand, what should we do?

Try to keep in tune with God's Spirit through prayer, fasting, and dedicated church activity, and draw guidance from gospel teachings that our parents and church instructors have given to us since childhood. If we do this, our spirit will prove to be "greater than this earth and sky," and we will be able to direct our controlled emotions into great works.

Summary

The kind of life we will have depends upon the type of decisions we make.

Losing control of our emotions can cause us to make unfavorable decisions.

Emotions, such as anxiety, can disrupt our ongoing behavior and prevent us from completing long-range tasks.

Keeping in tune with God's Spirit and applying gospel teachings will enable us to use our controlled emotions in doing great things.

16

How to Overcome Three Typical Emotional Problems

In the preceding chapter, an operational framework for managing emotions was presented. Suggestions for handling three typical problems that are emotionally oriented will be presented here. They are: destructive tensions, an inferiority complex, and a state of depression.

Combating Destructive Tensions

Sir William Osler, famous Canadian physician, once said, "It matters less what disease the patient has than what kind of patient has the disease."

The same thing is true of tensions. When people get tense and into hot water emotionally, some explode and others relax and take a bath, or, in other words, roll with the punches.

What is tension?

It is the body's reaction to stress. It can be constructive or destructive. It is constructive when it is converted into enjoyment with a purpose, such as the tension that precedes and the relaxation that follows giving a talk in church; the enjoyable tension that is associated with watching an exciting basketball game; the beneficial tension that warms up a person to run a footrace, or emerge victorious at table tennis, or fashion a new gown.

Tension is destructive when the overmobilized body does not go back to normal. The muscles remain too tight, blood pressure stays too high, the appetite is gone, and judgment is blurred. If this condition occurs frequently and severely and persists over a long period of time, it may cause problems, such as alcoholism, obesity, arthritis, ulcers, and other disorders.

We may also develop a low boiling point, and people may feel that they have to "walk on eggs" to get along with us.

If we don't let destructive tensions develop, we won't have to fight them. To stop them from developing we should—

1. Learn to be flexible under stress.

2. Allow other individuals to have their viewpoints and recognize why they think differently from us.

3. Not depend on one source for happiness and gratification; fill our emotional needs from associating with a variety of people and having a number of interests and activities.

4. Avoid taking ourselves too seriously, and accept our limitations and be ready to laugh at our harmless mistakes.

5. Keep involved in something that provides us with self-fulfillment and serves others.

To relieve tension, we might—

1. Organize our tasks into small workable units and give priority to the most urgent. For example, we will get more windows washed if we do the front ones first and a few each day, rather than attempting to do them all in one outburst of energy.

2. Not worry about bridges we may never cross.

3. If trying to make a decision is tearing us apart emotionally, walk away from it for awhile or sleep on it. Later, it may seem simpler to resolve.

4. Escape from routine tasks for awhile. If we get tense at work, we should stand up, breathe deeply, and exhale slowly—or, if circumstances permit, take a warm, leisurely bath, read a relaxing book, go to a movie, do something we like.

5. Find a hobby we enjoy.

6. Do something for someone else.

Getting Rid of That Inferiority Complex

People who come for counseling often try to excuse their lack of accomplishment or unhappiness by saying, "I have an inferiority complex."

How can we overcome one? The following things might help. We should—

1. Try not to feel inferior because we are not perfect. We wouldn't be on this earth if we were.

2. Quit trying to please all people. Discover our truest self and live accordingly. Others with similar traits will appreciate us.

3. Get over the idea that we have to be everything and do everything.

4. Strive to do our best work in some field that interests us and in which we have aptitude.

5. Do things that will give us satisfaction and that at the same time will benefit mankind.

6. Get acquainted with ourselves, see our imperfections, and correct them, if we can, but not brood about them.

7. Stand erect and tell ourselves out loud that we can accomplish a worthy, short-term goal and move toward our long-range goals.

8. Love ourselves so we can love others. If we don't love ourselves, because we feel we are not perfect, we

won't be able to love anyone else because we won't find a perfect person.

Overcoming Depression

A question that is repeatedly asked in the author's Personal Adjustment class is, "How can I overcome depression?"

I have answered many individuals by telling them the following true story.

A woman came for counseling who had been under psychiatric treatment for two years in an attempt to lift herself out of a depressed state. After some preliminary conversation, I asked her if she knew why she was depressed.

"Of course," she replied with some indignation. "I'm depressed because I am a very religious person and feel ashamed that I can't control my emotions."

"You mean you're depressed about your depression?" I asked.

"That's right," she said. "As a person who has deep faith in God and is an active church-goer, I have no right to get blue. I should be happy all the time."

"So," I countered, "you feel you should be above depression because you love God and try to do his will?"

"Certainly."

"Apparently you think you have more emotional control than did Jesus Christ, our Savior."

"Why do you say that?"

"If I remember the New Testament correctly, Christ was under emotional stress and probably unhappy several times during his life. One time, for example, was when he was praying in the Garden of Gethsemane. He knelt down and prayed, saying, 'Father, if thou wilt, remove this cup from me: nevertheless, not my will, but thine be done.'

"The scriptures say further, '. . . and being in agony, he prayed more earnestly: and his sweat was as if it were great drops of blood falling to the ground.'

"Do you want me to tell you about some other times when he seemed unhappy?"

"No, you've made your point."

"Well?"

"I feel better already, as if I've had a great load lifted from my shoulders. I realize now that I've been expecting too much of myself. You have really helped my spirits."

The sister left with a smile and never came back, so, assuming that no news is good news, she evidently overcame her depression.

Now, overcoming depression can't be done just by reading this story, but we can make a start by determining if we are expecting too much of ourselves.

Other things that can be done are:

1. Getting away from the environment associated with depression. This might include people and things.

2. Avoiding situations in which heavy demands are made on us. If we can't cope with a specific task or feel incompatible with a certain person, we should not try to resolve either problem until we feel a greater sense of adequacy.

3. Joining groups of people with problems similar to our own and, through mutual discussion, gaining emotional support.

4. Learning to break down our problems into smaller units and work on one unit at a time. We can accomplish wonders this way.

5. Thanking God for each new day and asking him to help us use it wisely.

Summary

Tensions can be converted into enjoyable and constructive activities.

Destructive tensions can be prevented by removing their causes.

Organizing our tasks into small, workable units will help reduce tensions.

As children of God we have no right to have an inferiority complex.

Thanking our Father in heaven for each new day and asking him to guide us through it is an antidote for depression.

17

This Moment Is
Ours to Enjoy

"Man must play, work, love and worship to get the most out of life." (Sir Wilfred Grenfell, famed English medical missionary.)

Are you happy this moment? Right now?

Or are you one of those future-livers who is putting up with life now and expecting your happiness when you reach the golden shores of heaven?

Don't be deceived—eternal happiness begins now. It comes from joy for the moment, which builds an enriched life, which leads to eternal happiness.

In other words, we must learn to be happy now if we expect to be happy in the hereafter.

Let me give you two illustrations:

Mrs. Smith is a good woman, a faithful church worker, whose only son, an outstanding young man, passed away in his early twenties. Since that time Mrs. Smith has simply endured this life, saying that she will never be happy again until she is reunited with her son.

Her face is always wreathed in sorrows and her chief topic of conversation is how happy she'll be when she can leave this dreary existence.

Mrs. Jones, another good woman and faithful church worker, has also been required to part with an only son. She has had many more earthly problems to cope with than Mrs. Smith, but her face is always wreathed in smiles, and she has an inner glow that brightens the lives of those around her. She revealed her formula for happiness one day in fast and testimony meeting when she said:

"When I arise each morning, I thank my Father in heaven for the privilege of enjoying another day and promise him that I will do my best to make it a good day. And you know, if you concentrate on making each day a good day, it's amazing how the days build into good weeks, good months, and good years.

"Of course I miss my son, but I know I'll be reunited with him eventually. In the meantime, there are too many things to enjoy right here to sit around and wait for future happiness."

To be happy, use the "KISS attitude."

Don't misunderstand! We're not suggesting that we'll enjoy each moment if we go around kissing everyone. It might be pleasant, at that, but in talking about the "KISS attitude," we mean something else. It is an attitude with two approaches which, if combined, will make each moment pleasurable.

Approach 1: At the University of Minnesota we recently had a basketball coach who was fabulously successful in getting the squad members to put out their best for him. His secret?

The "KISS attitude"—"Keep It Simple, Stupid."

Whenever he and the fellows were getting tense in a hotly contested game, he would grin and say, "KISS [Keep It Simple, Stupid]." This would break the fellows up with laughter, and they would relax and play better.

It helps to try this when some task seems difficult and perplexing: pause, take a deep breath, and say, "Keep It Simple, Stupid."

Surely life would be more fun if we would keep it simple by concentrating on one thing at a time. One writer put it this way: "Life by the yard is hard; by the inch, it's a cinch."

Some people might question the use of the word "stupid" in the formula. This is put there to enable us to laugh at our mistakes and realize that we're not perfect. Of course, individuals who are too dignified to refer to themselves as stupid can always substitute the words *sunbeam* or *saint*.

Approach 2: The best way to make and keep friends, which increases happiness, is to use "KISS attitude number two": "Kindness—Interest—Smile—Service."

Kindness is the basic message of the Bible. We are told, "Love thy neighbour," "He who loves God loves his brother, too."

We may be honored for our wisdom, but we will be loved for our kindness. And if we want affection in our lives, we must send it out first from ourselves.

Interest in others can give us many happy moments. A quick way to make friends is to ask people about their interests, their opinions, and their activities.

Marlene Dietrich, who has long been considered a charming and beautiful woman, once said, "The average man is more interested in a woman who is interested in him than a woman with a beautiful figure."

We will enjoy every moment with friends if we will listen to them with interest.

Smile. How does the song go? "Let a smile be your umbrella on a rainy, rainy day."

Greet the next person you meet with a smile, and see what happens. Smiles are infectious. They melt reserve in people like the sun melts ice on your sidewalk.

Service. Doing things for others is one of the best ways to make our life happy.

Specific Suggestions

Now let's look at some specific suggestions for enjoying each moment. We are not going to suggest a schedule to follow and then say, "Now enjoy." Because enjoyment must be spontaneous, it cannot be commanded.

But, here are a few ideas we might use.

1. Use our talents.

"Use what talents you possess. The woods would be very silent if no birds sang there except those that sang best." (Henry Van Dyke.)

We shouldn't be afraid to try new things. We won't be graded on our efforts.

If we like music, how about making some of our own? We may not sing as well as Dinah Shore or Robert Goulet, but we can sing anyway. And even if we have laryngitis and can't sing, we can always lift our spirits by listening to music.

If we have always had a yen to paint in oil, we should try it. Modern art allows such freedom of expression that one doesn't have to be a Grandma Moses or a Picasso to put impressions on a canvas.

Would you like to create an original gown? Visit a fabric shop, select some material you love, obtain a pattern, and get busy. If it doesn't turn out just right, who cares, as long as you enjoy it.

2. Collect things that give us joy.

So we can't afford a collection of expensive antiques or Dresden china; we can acquire other things that we enjoy.

How about—

—carrying snapshots of those we love in our purse? A snapshot not only brings us closer to them but may also recall happy times or special occasions.

—having an "album for ideas"? Proverbs, statements of great people, and observations of the thinking and actions of those around us can give us an album or book of ideas for living that may even be more valuable than a bankbook. To do this, it also helps to read the Bible and other great writings.

—collecting rocks, shells, driftwood, or any of the

things that nature gives so freely? Such hobbies can sharpen powers of observation and become an interesting part of our life.

3. Play at least one hour each day.

It has been said, "A great man or woman can become a child at will." How long has it been since you played jump-the-rope? drop the handkerchief? any kind of ball game? chess? checkers? anagrams? charades?

We should never get too old to play a little each day.

4. Rest.

Sit still in an easy chair and relax. Avoid picking up anything to read or something to do, but just meditate and daydream. These moments can become magic.

5. "Work with a will."

The words of this favorite religious song ("Today While the Sun Shines") are filled with meaning. We should find some work that we love, and rejoice that we are helping God keep this world going.

6. Make the day brighter for someone.

This can be done by writing a letter that says, "I miss you," "I am proud of you," "I love you." If you have ever been stationed in a far-away country, separated from family and friends, you know what such a letter means. A cheering letter is the reaching out of one spirit to another.

We can also remember an anniversary with a phone call, and visit someone who feels lonely.

7. Start and end each day talking to God.

Summary

Happiness is now! Each happy moment will
add up to an eternity of happiness.
Cultivate the two "KISS ATTITUDES."
Keep It Simple, Stupid,
and
Kindness—Interest—Smile—Service.
We can enjoy each moment by—
—using our talents,
—collecting things that give us joy,
—playing each day,
—resting some magic moments,
—working with a will,
—making the day brighter for someone, and
—talking with God.

Our Final Challenge As Children of God Is to—

—bring beauty and good to a sin-wracked world.

—be a light that dispels confusion and doubt and illuminates the pathway back to our Heavenly Father.

APPENDIX

Sources of Counseling

If we have problems that bother us, it usually helps to get our troubled thoughts out into the open by telling them to someone. At this moment, thousands of individuals are doing just that—pouring out their feelings to a listener via the telephone, over the back fence, in a barbershop, inside a church, or in some other setting.

Does it make any difference with whom we share our problems?

Indeed it does. It probably would not, if the conversation were a one-way street in which we did all of the talking. Then we could likely get as much relief from telling our troubles to a favorite pet.

However, this is not the case when we air our problems to humans. Each individual listener will react in his or her own special way. Some will criticize us. Others will offer too much sympathy, and a select few will react to our story with warmth and objective understanding. Because of the varied responses that we might receive, the possible solutions to our difficulties may be speeded up or slowed down by the reactions of our listener.

So, if we are lonely, discouraged, or just plain blue, and want help, we should use wisdom in selecting the person we confide in.

To give you assistance in locating your most effective source of counseling, let's assume you are trying to put your life together again after going through a divorce.

You may feel like Ruth A., who said, "My husband didn't contribute one red cent to our family budget for over two years, and I know he was running around with other women. Nevertheless, now that we are divorced and I am facing life alone, I find it desperately difficult to keep going. Although my husband was a noncontributing, part-time mate, he was better than none at all."

Ruth did find the courage to face her new life realistically and keep going, because she had the faith to seek her Heavenly Father's guidance and talked her problems over with understanding people. In so doing, she learned that some Church officers and members were more helpful than others, and through trial and error she found those who best helped her acquire the needed insights. She would have saved time and avoided some heartaches if she had known from the start which counselors would be best suited to help her with her particular needs.

Now, back to you. If you feel you want counseling, some sources to consider are given below. They are listed along with a summary of the services they offer. Knowing something about these sources may enable you to avoid random searching for the right counselor and go immediately to the most suitable person or persons for help.

LDS Church Counseling

Members of The Church of Jesus Christ of Latter-day Saints have a number of special sources to turn to for help.

The bishop, who acts as the father of the ward, is usually available for consultation day and night. He is always ready to give counsel, offer emotional support, and provide material assistance. This same kind of special counseling may be provided by your stake president (in the mission field, your branch, district, or mission president). Members should also feel free to talk to the Relief Society president or some other understanding sister.

Nevertheless, in some cases distressed members think they might feel uncomfortable if they tell their troubles to one of these Church workers. This may be because they look upon them as friends in whom it would be embarrassing to confide, or because they feel there is an age difference that might interfere with establishing rapport. Church leaders have sensed such possibilities, and as a result have established a Church Social Services department that is structured to help members with their social-emotional problems. Such services should now be available throughout the Church.

In this program, professionally trained counselors—men and women who have been called to the position by the stake president—are available. They are well equipped to discuss any problem you want to talk about.

Their services are also available to nonmembers.

Other Possible Sources of Counseling

In the event that it is not possible for geographical or other reasons to receive counseling within the framework of Church Social Services, other possible sources of counseling are listed below.

1. Relatives

It is natural to turn to relatives for help. And if we are trying to adjust or have any other problem, no one will be more genuinely interested in our welfare than an understanding relative.

Relatives usually stand ready to assist emotionally, financially, and socially. Just having a loved one listen and say, "I know how you feel; we all have difficult decisions to make, and faith and prayer will help us through them," is reassuring and supportive emotionally.

Good-hearted relatives may help economically with financial backing and in assisting with housing accommodations and job placement. They may also help make one's social life more interesting.

Yes, relatives can be good counselors. However, they sometimes make the situation worse by—

—"taking sides" between divorced partners or bickering sweethearts. For example, parents may feel that their darling daughter or favorite son could never do anything wrong, and the whole trouble must lie with the former husband or wife.

—being overprotective with us, thus hindering our growth.

—putting social pressures on us that may multiply our difficulties.

—telling our friends about our marriage break-up, thus making possible reconciliation more difficult.

—giving advice based on their experiences that may be totally unrelated to our problems.

Comment: Relatives do not always make effective counselors.

2. Friends

We may be fortunate in that we have friends in whom we can confide. But their suggestions may lack objectivity. Friends can—

—lend a listening ear around the clock.

—take a personal interest in our problems.

—support us with nonjudgmental encouragement.

However, friends sometimes make things worse by—

—seeing only our side of the situation.

—reinforcing our negative feelings by saying such things as "Put your foot down," "Let him know who's boss," and "He never was worthy of you!"

—confiding our problems to others.

Comment: Friends usually make better listeners than counselors.

3. Persons in the Media

Millions of dollars are paid each year to public advisers for personal counseling. These include persons associated with mass media, such as newspapers, magazines, and books.

We shouldn't believe everything we read. Gutenberg would roll over in his grave if he knew how his invention of the printing press has been used to exploit the public. It doesn't pay to place much faith in the ten easy questions found in newspapers, magazines, or books that supposedly guide one to marital or personal success. These clever "come-ons" have seldom been psychologically tested and are printed primarily to increase the publisher's circulation.

Advice columns can be of assistance in certain limited ways. They can offer consolation and reassurance, provide information, and give some insights to their readers.

Writing to such columnists for advice is therapeutically helpful in that it ventilates tensions and causes us to organize our thinking. The drawbacks of the columnist's answers may be that they are not geared to our particular personality. For example, the suggested solution may be one that will transcend one's capacity and thus increase feelings of inadequacy. The reason this may happen is because the columnist does not have a face-to-face relationship with us and is required to assess our personality from the written word.

Qualified personal adjustment counselors avoid such pitfalls by studying an individual in a face-to-face relationship and then usually help develop several optional courses of behavior to decide on.

Comment: We should use printed articles, columns, and books as aids to decision-making, not as prescriptions to follow.

The electronics media often produce excellent family programs that present sound personal and family attitudes to viewers. Also, other types of programs that demonstrate the actual process of marriage counseling can be of value. Still, there are at least three possible weaknesses in such presentations. First, because of time limitations the program may oversimplify the personal problem. Second, overdramatization may be engaged in to make it appealing. Third, the primary purpose of most of these programs is to sell products, not to help people.

Will going to a family-oriented film or play give an individual the insight needed to solve his problem?

It all depends on whether it can be viewed objectively. Ignoring the romantic trappings and sensing the writer's or producer's bias and focusing attention on the plot might be helpful.

Comment: Viewing a film or play may probably be of greatest therapeutic value if a group of interested people see it and then discuss it objectively.

4. Professional Counselors

Not every person who is a sympathetic listener qualifies as a counselor. Neither does every advice-giver. Consequently, pouring out one's troubles to a beautician, cab driver, or neighbor may either help or hinder adjustment.

These friendly nonprofessionals may be of considerable assistance if they listen in a nonjudgmental manner and avoid telling us what to do. But if we want the most effective guidance, we should be selective. Many ill-trained and unscrupulous individuals advertise themselves as professional counselors. Some use a crystal ball in dispensing advice. Others buy a diploma from a nonaccredited school.

The safest procedure to follow to procure a reliable counselor is to contact a nearby university or Community Chest organization to obtain names of recommended counselors.

Trained counselors come from several related fields, such as psychiatry, psychology, sociology, social work, home economics, nursing, medicine, the clergy, and the legal profession.

If you visit one, don't expect him or her to give you a magic formula for success or say, "After three interviews, I'll guarantee your troubles will be over." Such procedures have the earmarks of quackery.

The Trained Counselor's Procedure

Inasmuch as there are many different types of counseling, it is difficult to describe how a trained counselor proceeds. Some use nondirective therapy (listen and reflect your thinking). Others use directive counseling, role therapy, and so forth. The individual should choose one with whom he feels comfortable and who has a sincere interest in helping him.

Comment: The trained counselor assists you in making the decision that should be best for you. The time it takes to do this may vary in relation to your development of new insights and the degree of motivation you have to solve your problems.

Remember!

If you desire help, there are many individuals available to assist with your problems.

These sources of counseling help are available within the Church and without.

Latter-day Saints usually consult the bishop or branch president, and then find the most suitable counseling arrangement within the structure of the Church's Social Services.

INDEX